GORDON RAMSAY'S

just desserts

WITH **ROZ DENNY**

PHOTOGRAPHS BY **GEORGIA GLYNN SMITH**

QUADRILLE

Dedication

To my all-star dream team – chefs, front of house, backup support staff, and Carla Pastorino my personal assistant. Thank you for your enthusiasm and dedication.

Notes

• All spoon measures are level unless otherwise stated:

1 teaspoon = 5ml spoon; 1 tablespoon = 15ml spoon.

• Egg sizes are specified where they are critical, otherwise you can use either large or medium eggs. I recommend free-range eggs. If you are pregnant or in a vulnerable health group, avoid those recipes that contain raw egg whites or lightly cooked eggs.

• Ovens should be preheated to the specified temperature. Individual ovens can deviate by as much as 10°C from the setting, either way. Get to know your oven and use an oven thermometer to check its accuracy. My timings are given as guidelines, with a description of colour or texture where appropriate.

Publishing Director Anne Furniss
Consultant Art Director Helen Lewis
Project Editor Janet Illsley
Production Sarah Tucker
Design Assistant Katy Davis
Editorial Assistant Katie Ginn

First published in 2001 by
Quadrille Publishing Limited
Alhambra House
27-31 Charing Cross Road
London WC2H oLS

This paperback edition first published in 2003
Reprinted in 2003, 2004, 2005
10 9 8 7 6 5 4

Text © Gordon Ramsay
Photographs © Georgia Glynn Smith
Design and layout © Quadrille Publishing Limited

Cataloguing in Publication Data: a catalogue record for this book is available from the British Library.

ISBN 1 84400 019 2
Printed in Singapore

contents

introduction

'Life is uncertain ... eat dessert first'

ANON

My love affair with desserts began as a humble commis in the Paris kitchens of Guy Savoy. My first post was sandwiched between two sorbet machines. It was a time when I was trying to memorise not only lingua cucina, but also lingua franca – a necessary skill if I was to survive the initiation into a classic French kitchen. These sorbet machines were situated next to the main swing doors into the restaurant, which meant I also had to press myself flat against the wall during the service rush hours. So, I learnt to improve both my culinary skills and language as quickly as possible.

And what skills I learnt. Guy Savoy's menu featured as many desserts as starters and main courses, a reflection of his initial training as pastry chef at the Troisgros restaurant. After the first month – a period of serious learning in the school of hard knocks, literally – I began to enjoy what I was doing. My French improved and within a month I was promoted to run the pastry section on Saturday nights in the absence of the regular pastry chef. Quel honneur!

Pastry chefs occupy a very special place in the pecking order of a high flying restaurant kitchen, so this made me feel important. It was an honour I took very seriously. Pastry chefs work late shifts, generally starting at 1.30pm and on into the night – way after evening service has finished. However, I was so eager to get it all right 'on the night' that I would get in at 9am.

I would say that 95% of the customers at my restaurant in Chelsea choose a dessert, a staggering figure. One of the favourites is blood orange jelly served with orange flower water ice cream and a Financier on the side – it is naturally light and full of flavour. I take my dessert skills as seriously as I do all my cooking. Roasting fruits correctly is as important as cooking the perfect fillet of turbot, or canon of baby Pyrenean lamb.

Like most chefs, I am nostalgic about puddings with happy childhood memories, the sort my Mother would serve. So, I have devoted a chapter to these, giving each of them a unique twist to bring them into the 21st century. My creamy rice pudding uses Thai fragrant rice and is served with mango, for example. My crumble is a light affair of pan-roasted fruit scented with vanilla and a crisp, loose topping. Some of these are stand-alone desserts, others are best served with real custard, homemade ice cream or smooth thick cream.

Because desserts can be frivolous, I've included a few fun ideas too. My funky baked baby pineapples and softly set pannacottas with their sexy wobble should make you smile. Enthusiasts may like to copy our composite dessert – a sabayon-topped fruit gratin, little pannacotta, and hot raspberry soufflé – all served on one plate and all in miniature. As two of these are prepare-ahead chilled desserts, this isn't as difficult as it sounds.

I'd like to think that I have included something for everyone here. At least, I encourage you to master a few easy classics – perhaps roasted fruits, crème anglaise, chocolate ganache for truffles and possibly the little treacle tarts I made for Prime Minister Blair and President Putin. After all, desserts are pure pleasure – enjoy.

fruit

SYRUPS

Flavoured syrups, fruit coulis and glazes are the salad dressings of the dessert world. They moisten and add flavour to a variety of recipes. The basis for all my fruit 'infusions' is a simple stock syrup. I always have some to hand in the fridge – a mere trickle will perk up the simplest combination of fruits and it keeps for a good month. You can impart character by steeping whole spices or other flavourings in the stock syrup as it cools.

Flavoured stock syrups

Make up a quantity of Stock syrup (page 200) and measure 250ml for each flavoured syrup. (Keep some plain for versatile use.) Add your chosen flavouring(s) to the syrup just after boiling and set aside to infuse until cold.

If the syrup is infused with fresh herbs they should be removed before storing; whole spices and vanilla can be retained for a stronger flavour. Store stock syrup in a screw-topped jar or bottle in the fridge; it will keep for 3–4 weeks.

Choose from the following:

For each of these, you need 250ml Stock syrup (page 200):

SPICED Add 1 strip of lemon zest, ½ teaspoon black peppercorns, 1 star anise, 1 small cinnamon stick and 1 clove.

VANILLA Add 1 vanilla pod, slit lengthways.

CITRUS Add 1 long, wide strip each of orange, lemon and either lime or grapefruit zest.

MINT, BASIL OR THYME Add a strip of lemon zest, plus 2 large sprigs of fresh spearmint, basil or thyme.

LEMON GRASS Add 1 large fresh lemon grass stalk, slit lengthways, plus a strip of lime zest.

HIBISCUS Add 2 teaspoons of dried hibiscus flowers (available from healthfood shops), or 2 rosehip and hibiscus tea bags.

COFFEE Add 2 teaspoons roasted coffee beans, plus 1 tablespoon white rum if liked.

LIQUEUR Add 2–3 tablespoons of your favourite – mine are Malibu, Kahlua and Amaretto. Or flavour with Grand Marnier, kirsch, brandy or rum.

COULIS AND GLAZES

These are simply fresh fruit purées thinned with stock syrup, to use as light sauces (coulis) or to spoon over sliced fruits in flans or fruit salads (as glazes). You can vary the flavours by using different syrups. Most fruits can be puréed raw, but a few will need to be cooked lightly first. The fruit must be nicely ripe, but not overripe or the coulis won't be fresh tasting. Purée the fruit with the small amount of syrup in a food processor or blender until smooth and runny, then rub through a sieve into a bowl with the back of a ladle. Freeze any you don't need at once in ice cube trays for later use.

Flooding a plate with coulis

Slices of fruit, parfait, tart etc, look attractive served with a pool of coulis. If possible, use wide shallow bowls so the coulis doesn't form a tide mark as you serve it. Have the coulis in a jug. Pour about 4–5 tablespoons into the centre of each bowl and tap the edge gently to level out the coulis.

Napping with a fruit sauce

We use this term to describe glazing or coating an item, such as fruit, with sauce. You simply take a large tablespoonful of coulis, hold it close over the item, then tip the spoon sideways so the sauce flows out and 'naps' it.

STRAWBERRY COULIS Purée 250g hulled fruits with a squeeze of lemon juice. Blend with 4 tablespoons Hibiscus, Lemon grass or Mint syrup (see left). Rub through a sieve.

KIWI COULIS Peel 4 kiwi fruit and purée with a squeeze of lime juice. Blend with 4–6 tablespoons Lemon grass syrup (see left), then rub through a sieve.

MANGO COULIS Peel and chop 2 ripe, medium mangoes. Purée with 4 tablespoons Spiced or Citrus syrup (see left) and 1 tablespoon lemon or orange juice. Rub through a sieve. A teaspoon of orange flower water will enhance the flavour.

RASPBERRY COULIS Purée 250g ripe raspberries, then blend with 4 tablespoons Lemon grass, Spiced or Mint syrup (see left). Add a splash of Drambuie too, if you like. Sieve to remove seeds.

PASSION FRUIT COULIS Halve 4 ripe, well-wrinkled passion fruit and scoop the pulp and seeds into a blender. Add 6 tablespoons Stock syrup (page 200) or Citrus syrup (see left) and blitz for some time until the seeds are well crushed. Rub through a sieve. As this coulis is quite pungent, you may prefer it mixed with strawberry purée or let down with some fresh orange juice.

PLUM OR CHERRY COULIS Stone about 200g plums or cherries. Purée, then blend with 4 tablespoons Spiced syrup (see left) or plain Stock syrup (page 200). Rub through a sieve. A tablespoon of brandy or kirsch is a good addition.

ORANGE AND PINK GRAPEFRUIT COULIS Squeeze the juices from 4 large oranges and 1 pink grapefruit. Strain into a small saucepan, add a sprig of fresh mint or lemon balm and boil until reduced by about a third. Skim off any scum from the surface with a slotted spoon. Add 1–2 teaspoons caster sugar to sweeten. Mix $^3/_4$ teaspoon cornflour to a smooth paste with 1 tablespoon of cold water, then mix in the citrus juice. Return to the pan and cook, stirring, until thickened. Cool, stirring once or twice. Discard the herb sprig.

BLACKCURRANT COULIS Top and tail 250g ripe blackcurrants. Simmer with 6 tablespoons plain Stock syrup (page 200) and a fresh mint sprig until tender; cool. Discard the mint, then purée in a food processor or blender. Rub through a sieve.

RHUBARB COULIS Chop 300g rhubarb and cook with 6 tablespoons plain Stock syrup (page 200) until soft. Cool and purée, then rub through a sieve. For a pretty pink colour, add a teaspoon or two of Grenadine.

APPLE OR PEAR COULIS Quarter, core and chop 400g fruit, but do not peel. Cook with 3 tablespoons plain Stock syrup (page 200) or Spiced syrup (page 10) and a good squeeze of lemon or lime juice. Cool, then purée and rub through a sieve.

In the restaurant, we also serve a light jus of Granny Smith as a coulis. This is simply a purée of freshly chopped Granny Smith apples, sharpened with a teaspoon of lemon juice, then pressed through a sieve with the back of a ladle, to extract as much natural juice as possible.

Mango and mint salsa

MAKES ABOUT 300g
1 large, just ripe mango
2 tablespoons Stock syrup (page 200)
1 tablespoon lemon juice
2 tablespoons chopped fresh mint

This tangy, textured fruit sauce is wonderful with creamy ices. In particular, I like to serve it with Nougat parfait (page 67). It can be kept in the fridge for up to 2 days.

1 Peel the mango and slice the flesh away from the stone, then chop finely.
2 Mix the syrup and lemon juice together in a bowl. Add the mango and toss to mix. Add the chopped mint just before serving.

Marinated cherries

We find so many uses for these that we make them in quantity when there is a reasonably priced glut, such as during late summer. I love the light red English cherries, but you can use dark red American ones. Obviously, the cherries are more versatile if stoned prior to macerating. Allow time for this – and make sure you have a good cherry stoner.

MAKES ABOUT 350g
500g ripe cherries
350ml Spiced syrup (page 10), or plain Stock syrup (page 200)
2–3 tablespoons kirsch

1 Stone the cherries – over a pan so you don't lose any juice. Pour the stock syrup into the pan and bring to the boil. Add the cherries and boil for 2 minutes. Remove from the heat and stir in the kirsch.
2 Spoon the hot cherries into a warm preserving jar, using a slotted spoon, then top up with the hot syrup. Seal and store in a cool, dark spot for up to 2 months. Use as required.

Variation

For freshly marinated cherries, make up some Blackcurrant coulis (see left) and add 2 3 tablespoons kirsch. Stone about 300g fresh cherries and place in a bowl. Bring the coulis to the boil in a saucepan, pour over the cherries and leave until cold. Cover and chill until ready to serve.

Macerated fruits

In the restaurant we steep dried fruits in hot rum and stock syrup and employ them in a variety of different ways. One of my favourite uses is to stir the rum-soaked fruits into homemade Vanilla or Cardamom ice cream (pages 57–8). You won't need all of this recipe for one quantity of ice cream, but you can leave the remaining fruits in the syrup and store them in the fridge – ready to spoon out whenever needed. Try them stirred into thick creamy Greek yogurt, too.

Steep the fruits at least 24 hours before you need them. They will keep for up to 4 weeks in the fridge.

MAKES 700g
500g raisins
100g currants
100g sultanas
500ml dark rum
100ml white rum
150ml Stock syrup (page 200)

1 Simply put all the fruits into a large saucepan with the dark and light rums and stock syrup. Slowly bring to the boil, then remove from the heat and leave to cool.
2 Decant into a large clean screw-topped jar. Leave the fruits to steep for at least 24 hours before scooping them out to use.

COMPOTES

A compote is a simple, thick purée of cooked or raw fruit, which we use as a base for fruit tarts, spoon into hot soufflés, or layer with a flavoured cream or yogurt in small glasses. In essence, a posh purée. A tip I learnt from Guy Savoy in Paris is that you must use slightly overripe fruit, as the natural fruit sugars will be at their best and your compote will need little, if any extra sugar. Needless to say, this is an excellent use for fruit that is just a little too soft to slice or dice. Serving quantities will depend on how the compote is to be used.

I like to present compotes in shot glasses or small wine glasses. To serve, put a heaped tablespoon of compote into each glass and spoon over some slightly sweetened Greek yogurt. Finally, top with a few shavings of fruit sorbet or granita, or a thin float of cream and perhaps a sprinkling of crushed honeycomb. Tell your guests to push their spoon right to the base of the glass – to savour all three layers at once.

Apricot compote

MAKES ABOUT 400ml
500g ripe apricots
25g butter
2 tablespoons caster sugar
2 star anise

SERVE IN SMALL GLASSES TOPPED WITH LEMON AND LIME CREAM (PAGE 52) AND A SPRINKLING OF LEMON AND LIME ZEST CONFIT STRIPS (PAGE 47)

1 Halve and stone the apricots, then cut into quarters. Melt the butter with the sugar in a heavy-based saucepan over a low heat and cook until it turns a light caramel colour.
2 Add the apricots and star anise. Cover the surface with a scrunched-up sheet of wet greaseproof paper. (This will allow some of the steam to escape, so the fruit is sautéed rather than stewed.) Cook on a medium heat for 10–15 minutes until very soft. Discard the star anise.
3 Now, off the heat, take a Bamix or stick blender to the pan and whizz the fruit to a purée. (Or purée in a food processor or blender.) Cool and chill until ready to use.

Pear and saffron compote

MAKES ABOUT 400ml

100ml poire eau-de-vie

3 large ripe pears, such as Conference,
    Williams or Comice, about 600g in total

25g butter

3 tablespoons caster sugar

¼ teaspoon saffron strands, crushed

Fragrant, juicy pears – enhanced with a hint of saffron – make an excellent compote. Lemon and lime cream (page 52) is the ideal complement.

1 Boil the eau-de-vie in a small saucepan until reduced by half, then set aside to cool (see note).

2 Quarter, core and peel the pears, then cut into large chunks. Melt the butter and sugar in a heavy-based saucepan over a low heat and cook to a light caramel colour. Toss in the pears and crushed saffron strands and cook, uncovered, for about 5 minutes.

3 Then cover the fruit with a crumpled sheet of wet greaseproof paper (rather than a lid, so that steam can still escape). Cook on a medium heat for a further 10 minutes or so, until the pears are soft.

4 Take off the heat and blend to a purée with the eau-de-vie, either in the pan with a Bamix or stick blender, or using a food processor or electric blender. Cool and use as required.

Note: You could use 50ml Poire William liqueur in place of the reduced eau-de-vie.

Apple and cranberry compote

MAKES ABOUT 400ml

500g apples, such as Granny Smith, Braeburn or
    Bramley's

40g butter

3 tablespoons caster sugar

1 cinnamon stick

125g fresh or frozen cranberries

LAYER IN GLASSES WITH THICK CREAMY
YOGURT AND A FLOAT OF SINGLE CREAM

I like to use this tangy purée as a base for an apple flan. It's a pretty shade of pink and is also good layered with thick yogurt and a little single cream – to serve as a light dessert around Christmas time. Granny Smith, Braeburn and Bramley apples all have a nice sweet/sharp balance of flavour, though you may need to add a little more sugar if you use Bramley's.

1 Quarter the apples, then remove the cores and peel. Cut into chunks. Heat the butter and sugar in a heavy-based saucepan over a low heat until melted and cook until it becomes a light caramel colour. Stir in the apples, add the cinnamon stick and cook, uncovered, for 5 minutes.

2 Stir in the cranberries and cover the surface with a sheet of crumpled wet greaseproof paper. Cook for a further 10 minutes until softened.

3 Discard the cinnamon stick, then purée in the pan with a Bamix or stick blender, or use a food processor or electric blender. Cool and use as required.

FRUIT SOUPS

Served chilled as a light dessert, these recipes may come as something of a surprise. Basically, they are thin fruit purées embellished with sliced or chopped fruits, and perhaps a small scoop of creamy ice cream or refreshing sorbet in the centre. Vanilla ice cream (page 57), of course, complements all soups. Fromage frais sorbet (page 76) and Pink grapefruit sorbet (page 78) are good palate-cleansers.

Peach soup with mint or lemon balm

In midsummer I prefer to use white peaches in my kitchen when they are at their best. But I know it's not always possible to get hold of them, so use any full-flavoured variety that happens to be available, even nectarines. This soup has a base of stock syrup and Champagne, let down with a little crème de pêche. A scattering of fresh raspberries or sliced strawberries provides a delicious contrast. As a final flourish, top with a scoop of ice cream or sorbet.

1 Halve the peaches and remove the stones. Place in a large saucepan and pour over the stock syrup and Champagne or wine. Add the cinnamon stick and cloves. Bring slowly to the boil, then partially cover and simmer for about 18 minutes until the fruit is just soft.

2 Take off the heat and stir in the mint or lemon balm sprigs. Set aside to cool and infuse.

3 Discard the cinnamon, cloves and herb sprigs. Drain the fruit into a sieve over a bowl; reserve the liquid.

4 Tip the fruit into a blender or food processor and whizz to a smooth pulp. Slowly mix in the reserved liquid until you have a light purée, the consistency of a thin soup; you may not need to add all of it. Whizz in the crème de pêche if using, then the cream. Pass through a sieve into a bowl and chill before serving.

5 Divide the fruit soup between 4 chilled soup plates and spoon the raspberries or strawberries in the centre.

SERVES 4-6

6–8 ripe peaches, depending on size

400ml light Stock syrup (page 200)

200ml Champagne, or sparkling white wine

1 cinnamon stick

2 cloves

2 large fresh mint or lemon balm sprigs

2 tablespoons crème de pêche (optional, but strongly recommended)

3 tablespoons double cream

125g raspberries, or sliced small strawberries, to serve

EXCELLENT TOPPED WITH A SCOOP OF STRAWBERRY SORBET (PAGE 72) OR FROMAGE FRAIS SORBET (PAGE 76)

Strawberry jus soup with cracked black pepper

SERVES 4–6

1kg ripe strawberries, hulled

1 tablespoon caster sugar

1 vanilla pod

3 mint leaves

1 tablespoon icing sugar, sifted

1–2 teaspoons coarsely ground or cracked
    black pepper

This light clear soup of strawberry juice could be described as a fruit consommé. But is it a first course or dessert? The answer is it can be both, though for a starter I wouldn't recommend topping it with ice cream. It's a good recipe to make when homegrown strawberries are at their peak and reasonably priced. And just as melon can be enhanced with a fiery spike of ginger, so strawberries get a kick from black pepper.

1 Set aside a third of the strawberries, selecting the firmest ones.
2 Cut up the rest of the fruit and place in a large heatproof bowl set over a pan of simmering water. Sprinkle with the caster sugar. Slit the vanilla pod open and scrape out the seeds, adding them to the bowl along with the mint leaves.
3 Cover the bowl with cling film and keep it over the pan for 30–40 minutes. This encourages the strawberries to exude their juice. Remove from the heat, cool and chill thoroughly for 2–3 hours.
4 About 30 minutes before serving, pour the jus into a sieve over a bowl and allow it to drip through; don't rub the pulp. Meanwhile place the reserved strawberries in a shallow bowl, sprinkle with the icing sugar and leave until they start to bleed.
5 Divide the strawberries between 4 chilled soup plates. Sprinkle lightly with the pepper and pour the chilled jus around them to serve.

FABULOUS TOPPED WITH A SCOOP OF
CHOCOLATE AND THYME ICE CREAM (PAGE
61) AS ILLUSTRATED, OR MORE SUBTLE
FROMAGE FRAIS SORBET (PAGE 76)

Plum soup with star anise

SERVES 4

500g ripe dark red plums

300ml light Stock syrup (page 200)

1 cinnamon stick

2 star anise

I love the deep burgundy colour of this soup. Make it in early autumn with homegrown plums that have been left to ripen on the tree. At other times plums can be quite a disappointment – all looks and little flavour.

1 Set aside a quarter of the firmer plums.
2 Halve, stone and slice the rest of the fruit and place in a saucepan. Pour over the stock syrup and add the cinnamon and star anise. Bring to the boil, then remove from the heat and leave until cool.
3 Discard the whole spices, then purée the fruit and syrup in a blender or food processor until smooth. Pass through a sieve into a bowl, rubbing with the back of a ladle. Chill until required.
4 Halve, stone and slice the reserved plums. Pour the soup into 4 soup plates and add the reserved plum slices.

SERVE TOPPED WITH A SCOOP OF VANILLA
OR CARDAMOM ICE CREAM (PAGES 57–8),
OR DRIZZLED WITH POURING CREAM

FRUIT SALADS

Fruit desserts suit my style. They are light and invigorating, with a good balance of acidity and sweetness. Fruits are also best served simply, to appreciate their sheer beauty. A selection of freshly prepared fruit dressed lightly with stock syrup makes an eye-catching and refreshing dessert. But do consider the colours and shapes. Fruits of the same hue make the most appealing salads – such as subtle combinations of green fruits, citrus fruits, red berries, or orange and gold tropical varieties – with perhaps one contrasting fruit.

Red berries with hibiscus and basil syrup

SERVES 4

150ml light Stock syrup (page 200)

1 tablespoon lemon juice

1 teaspoon dried hibiscus flowers, or 2 rosehip
   and hibiscus tea bags

2 large fresh basil leaves

300g small raspberries

125–200g wild strawberries, or very small
   cultivated ones, hulled

tiny fresh basil leaves, to serve

TRULY REFRESHING SERVED WITH
FROMAGE FRAIS SORBET (PAGE 76) OR
PINK GRAPEFRUIT SORBET (PAGE 78)

Small wild strawberries are exquisite coupled with fresh raspberries in a deep ruby red syrup, scented with hibiscus flowers. Wild strawberries are expensive to buy, but they do grow freely in even the smallest town garden, so consider potting up a few plants – they come up year after year. As for the basil, it goes really well with red berry fruits.

1 Bring the stock syrup almost to the boil and stir in the lemon juice, hibiscus flowers or tea bags, and basil leaves. Take off the heat and leave to infuse for about 20 minutes. Strain and set aside until required.
2 About 10 minutes before serving, place the raspberries and strawberries in a bowl, add the infused syrup and stir gently; don't over-stir or the fruit will break up. Leave to macerate for 10 minutes.
3 Serve in individual bowls, topped with basil leaves.

Minted melon salad

A selection of melons, scooped into balls and enhanced with a clove and mint syrup, makes a wonderfully refreshing dessert for a hot summer's day. It's good for a special brunch too. My choice of melons gives a subtle variation in flavour, sweetness and colour. Checking the fruit for ripeness requires sniffing and gentle thumb pressure applied at the stalk end. We tend to buy melons a few days ahead when they are fragrant but still quite firm, and let them ripen alongside a bunch of bananas.

1 Heat the stock syrup in a pan until almost boiling, then add the cloves, remove from the heat and set aside to infuse until cool.
2 Prepare the melons. Halve the whole fruit and deseed all the melons. Scoop the flesh into balls using a melon baller and place in a bowl. Pour over the cooled syrup and leave to macerate for 10 minutes. Discard the cloves.
3 Finely shred the mint leaves and gently stir into the melon salad. Leave to stand for a further 5 minutes, then serve.

SERVES 4–6
200ml light Stock syrup (page 200)
2 cloves
1 small Ogen or ½ honeydew melon
1 small Charentais melon
1 wedge of watermelon, about 400g
about 6–8 large mint leaves

ALLURING SCATTERED WITH SHAVINGS OF LEMON GRASS GRANITA (PAGE 82) AS ILLUSTRATED

Exotic fruit salad with fresh coconut

In general I'm not keen on clashing colours in fruit salads but this one will put your guests in a tropical mood. Choose either a citrus or spiced stock syrup and add a good splash of rum, or Angostura's for a less alcoholic kick. Search out a young, fresh coconut – Asian food stores sometimes have them. Open the coconut with a hammer and grate some of the flesh to use as a topping for the fruit salad.

1 Mix the cooled flavoured stock syrup with the rum or Angostura Bitters.
2 Prepare all the fruits, peeling and coring, stoning or deseeding as necessary. Cut or slice into bite-size pieces, but don't chop them all up equally – take advantage of their natural shapes. Place all the prepared fruits in a bowl.
3 Add the flavoured syrup, mix gently and leave to macerate for about 20 minutes. Meanwhile, peel the skin from the coconut and coarsely grate about 3–4 tablespoons of flesh.
4 Sprinkle the grated coconut over the fruit salad to serve.

SERVES 6
300ml Spiced or Citrus light stock syrup (page 10), cooled
3–4 tablespoons white rum, or few shakes of Angostura Bitters
1 medium pineapple
1 mango
1 papaya (pawpaw)
1 large peach, or 2 apricots
1 Asian pear (nashi)
1 star fruit
2 kiwi fruit
125g strawberries
small chunk of fresh coconut, to serve

CUMIN SHORTBREADS (PAGE 172) AND LADY'S FINGERS (PAGE 174) ARE APPROPRIATE ACCOMPANIMENTS

Bananas in caramel rum syrup

SERVES 4

150g caster sugar

230ml water

juice of 1 lemon

2–3 tablespoons white rum or Malibu

1 vanilla pod

1 cinnamon stick

2 star anise

4 large, just ripe bananas

SERVE AS A STAND-ALONE DESSERT, OR AS A LUSCIOUS ACCOMPANIMENT TO A PARFAIT, MOUSSE OR BAVAROIS

Bananas steeped in a rich syrup with a hint of vanilla and spices. For a lively kick, I suggest adding white rum or my favourite treat, Malibu – then close your eyes and imagine a tropical beach. Choose bananas that are firm and only just ripe.

1 Put the sugar and 2 tablespoons of the water in a large shallow pan over a gentle heat, stirring once or twice until dissolved. When the sugar syrup is clear, raise the heat and cook to a light caramel, about 5 minutes.

2 Immediately remove from the heat, cool for 2 minutes then stir in the lemon juice, taking care as it will spit a little. Mix in the rum or Malibu and remaining 200ml water. Slit the vanilla pod lengthways and add to the syrup with the whole spices.

3 Peel the bananas and halve lengthways. Place in a single layer in the pan and spoon the caramel syrup over to coat them all over; this also prevents the bananas from discolouring.

4 Leave to macerate for 40 minutes before serving. A flavoured crème fraîche, such as lemon grass or ginger (page 50), is a nice complement.

JELLIES

Simple concoctions of freshly prepared fruit and pure fruit juice, lightly set in crystal clear dishes, make mouth-watering desserts. My jellies are not for moulding because I prefer a softer set. If you want to set them in terrines or individual moulds for turning out, then increase the quantity of gelatine by about a quarter.

All jellies and terrines made in my restaurant kitchen are set with leaf gelatine. Quite simply, this is easier to use than powdered gelatine. You can buy leaf gelatine from selected supermarkets and good delis. Allow 4–5 sheets of gelatine per 500ml of total liquid in a recipe, depending on the other ingredients that are included. For example, if there is whipped cream in a recipe, you won't need quite as much gelatine.

Gelatine isn't suitable for vegetarians because it is derived from animal protein, but a vegetarian setting agent derived from the seaweed, agar-agar is available. Like cornflour and arrowroot, it is first mixed with liquid then gently heated, stirring until smooth. However the set is different from that obtained with gelatine and somewhat less stable.

One final point, gelatine is made from animal protein and is broken down by certain fruit enzymes found in pineapple, papaya and kiwi. So, if you are creating your own jelly recipes, avoid these fruits or serve them separately as a coulis or salad. I also find that very acidic fruits will need a little extra gelatine.

To use leaf gelatine

1 Immerse the sheets of leaf gelatine in a bowl of cold water for about 5 minutes to soften (breaking them in half to fit in the bowl if necessary).

2 Drain the leaf gelatine sheets and squeeze out excess water with your hands.

3 Slip the transparent sheets into the hot liquid (as per the recipe), whisking as you do so.

4 Whisk thoroughly until the leaf gelatine has melted completely.

5 As a precaution, pass the liquid through a sieve to ensure there are no traces of undissolved gelatine.

Using powdered gelatine

Allow one 11g sachet for each 500–600ml of the total liquid in the recipe (one sachet is roughly equivalent to 4–6 sheets of leaf gelatine). Sprinkle small amounts (up to 1 sachet) into the just-boiled liquid, stirring briskly to dissolve until the liquid becomes clear.

If using more than one sachet, you will first need to soften the crystals. Put 3–5 tablespoons cold water in a small bowl, sprinkle on the gelatine and leave to stand for about 5 minutes. To dissolve, stand the bowl in a small pan of simmering water until clear, or in the microwave on a low setting. Slowly incorporate into the hot liquid (as per recipe).

Strawberry and pink Champagne jelly

SERVES 8

600g strawberries, hulled

100g caster sugar

juice of 1 lemon

8 sheets of leaf gelatine

75cl bottle pink Champagne or sparkling rosé

2 tablespoons crème de pêche

TO SERVE:

double cream

This terrific summer pudding merits a good bottle of pink bubbly. The Champagne bubbles add a pretty prickle as you bite into the soft melting texture. Sarge, one of my enthusiastic sous chefs, developed the novel presentation idea. A fun choice for a party.

1 Slice 500g of the strawberries and place in a large heatproof bowl over a pan of gently simmering water. Stir in the sugar and lemon juice.

2 Cover the bowl with cling film and leave it like this for 30–40 minutes, checking the water in the pan occasionally and topping up with boiling water as necessary. The fruits will yield a clear pink fragrant jus.

3 Meanwhile, line a large sieve with wet muslin and place over a clean bowl. Pour the strawberry jus into the sieve and leave it to drip through, but don't rub the pulp otherwise the jus will lose its clarity. Discard the fruit pulp.

4 Soften the gelatine sheets in cold water (see pages 26–7). Meanwhile, pour the strawberry jus into a clean pan and heat until on the point of boiling then take off the heat. Remove the gelatine from the cold water, squeezing out excess water and then slip into the hot jus, whisking until dissolved. Pass through a sieve into a bowl.

5 Allow to cool, then mix in the Champagne and crème de pêche. Leave until the jelly is cold and just on the point of setting.

6 Meanwhile, slice the remaining 100g strawberries. Have ready 8 wine glasses or Champagne flutes. Dip the strawberry slices quickly into a little of the setting jelly and stick to the side of the glasses.

7 Now for the fun bit. To make this jelly sparkle, whisk the setting jelly until lightly frothy and divide it between the glasses. Chill until completely set.

8 To serve, top with a thin float of double cream, or a layer of raspberry cream and a spoonful of whipped cream. Keep it simple.

EXQUISITE TOPPED WITH RASPBERRY CREAM (PAGE 51) AND A SPOONFUL OF WHIPPED CREAM

Raspberry and lemon grass jelly

SERVES 6

500g raspberries

100g caster sugar

juice of 1 lemon

2 tablespoons crème de framboise

500ml water

150ml dry white wine

3 lemon grass stalks, sliced

6 sheets of leaf gelatine

TO SERVE:

double cream

SET IN ELEGANT WINE GLASSES TOPPED
WITH RASPBERRY CREAM (PAGE 51) OR
WHIPPED CREAM

This is made in the same way as the Strawberry and pink Champagne jelly (on page 28). You need to use full-flavoured ripe raspberries, preferably homegrown.

1 Place the raspberries, sugar, lemon juice and framboise in a large heatproof bowl over a pan of gently simmering water.

2 Cover the bowl with cling film and leave it to warm for 30–40 minutes until you have a clear pink jus, checking the water in the pan occasionally and topping up with boiling water as necessary. Strain the jus through a sieve lined with wet muslin into a bowl, but don't be tempted to rub the pulp otherwise the jus will turn cloudy. Discard the fruit pulp.

3 Meanwhile, bring the water and wine to the boil in a saucepan. Stir in the lemon grass, take off the heat and set aside to infuse until cold. Strain the liquor and discard the lemon grass.

4 Soften the gelatine sheets in cold water (see pages 26–7). Reheat the raspberry jus in a clean pan until on the point of boiling and mix with the infused wine liquor.

5 Lift out the gelatine sheets and squeeze to remove excess water. Off the heat, add them to the raspberry jus mixture and whisk to dissolve. Pass through a sieve into a bowl.

6 Leave until cold and on the point of setting. Divide between 6 glasses and chill until completely set.

7 Float a little double cream on top of each jelly to serve.

Blueberry and thyme jelly

This darker jelly looks enticing set in fine wine glasses. It is also fabulous layered in tall glasses, either with the Strawberry and pink Champagne jelly (page 28), or the Raspberry and lemon grass jelly (see left). Try this for a special occasion, allowing time for each layer to set before you add the next one.

1 Place the berries in a large heatproof bowl over a pan of gently simmering water. Stir in 50g of the sugar and the lemon juice.

2 Cover the bowl with cling film and leave it like this for 30–40 minutes, checking the water in the pan occasionally and topping up with boiling water as necessary. The fruits will yield a clear dark jus.

3 Meanwhile, put the water and remaining 25g sugar in a saucepan and dissolve over a low heat. Add the thyme sprigs and lemon grass and bring to the boil. Take off the heat and set aside to infuse for 1 hour. Strain the liquor into a jug and discard the flavourings.

4 Pass the berry jus through a muslin-lined sieve into a clean bowl, but don't rub the pulp with the back of a spoon otherwise the jus will lose its clarity; discard the fruit pulp.

5 Soften the gelatine sheets in cold water (see page 26–7). Meanwhile, pour the berry jus into a clean pan, add the infused liquid and heat until on the point of boiling. Take off the heat.

6 Remove the gelatine from the cold water, squeezing out excess water and then slip into the hot jus mixture, whisking until dissolved. Pass through a sieve into a bowl.

7 Leave until the jelly is cold and just on the point of setting. Divide between serving glasses and chill until completely set.

8 Float a little double cream on top of each jelly to serve.

SERVES 4–6

300g blueberries
100g blackberries
75g caster sugar
juice of 1 lemon
500ml water
3 large fresh thyme sprigs
2 lemon grass stalks, sliced
5 sheets of leaf gelatine
TO SERVE:
double cream

SET IN TALL GLASSES LAYERED WITH A CONTRASTING JELLY, OR SERVE SIMPLY TOPPED WITH A FLOAT OF CREAM

Blood orange jelly

MAKES 4

12 blood oranges

1 pink grapefruit

4 sheets of leaf gelatine

4 tablespoons Stock syrup (page 200)

2 tablespoons Campari

TO SERVE:

double cream

SERVED TOPPED WITH A FLOAT OF CREAM
AND ACCOMPANIED BY FINANCIERS
(PAGE 173)

This is the hot favourite in my restaurant during the summer, especially with the ladies. Blood oranges have a unique flavour and their pretty segments – set in a light jelly made from the juice – makes a stunning dessert. We set these jellies in attractive cocktail glasses and serve them with Orange flower water ice cream (page 59) and a trickle of Passion fruit coulis (page 11). Here they are simply topped with a float of single cream, and served with a Financier (page 173) on the side.

1 Finely pare thin strips of zest from 2 oranges. Peel and segment 4 oranges and the grapefruit (see below). Squeeze the juice from the remaining oranges; you should have about 700ml.

2 Immerse the gelatine sheets in a bowl of cold water for about 5 minutes until floppy.

3 Meanwhile, put the orange juice in a saucepan with the zest strips and stock syrup and bring to the boil. Take off the heat.

4 Remove the gelatine from the cold water, squeezing out excess water, then slide into the hot orange juice, whisking until dissolved. Pass through a sieve into a bowl and add the Campari. Set aside to cool for 30 minutes.

5 Meanwhile, divide half the fruit segments between 4 serving glasses. Spoon a little of the juice mixture over the segments and chill until set.

6 Add the remaining segments, then pour over the rest of the orange juice. Refrigerate for a good 2 hours until the jelly is lightly set.

To segment an orange (or other citrus fruit)

1 Using a small sharp knife, slice the top and bottom from the orange, removing the white pith as well.

2 Standing the orange upright, slice off all the peel and pith cutting downwards and following the contours of the fruit so you don't take off too much flesh. You should end up with a neat, rounded shape.

3 Hold the orange in one hand over a bowl to catch the juice and cut each side of the membranes that contain the segments to release them. As each segment is loosened, slip it into the bowl. When you have removed all the segments, give the spent membrane a squeeze to extract any remaining juice.

ROASTED FRUITS

Cooking fruit at a high heat caramelises the flesh and imparts a sweet char-grilled flavour that is deliciously different. You can do this in two ways – either in a preheated heavy-based non-stick frying pan, or in a hot oven basting from time to time with a little syrup, alcohol or both. I sometimes add herb sprigs such as thyme and rosemary too.

Slow roasted peaches with orange caramel sauce

SERVES 6

250g caster sugar

3 tablespoons water

250ml fresh orange juice

1 vanilla pod

6 medium white peaches

50g unsalted butter, softened until runny but not melted

TO FINISH (OPTIONAL):

Sugar-crusted basil leaves (page 71)

You need to roast these peaches whole and unskinned, basting them from time to time with the orange caramel sauce. The texture holds up nicely and the flavour is so good.

1 Put 150g of the sugar and the water in a heavy-based saucepan and dissolve over a low heat. When the sugar syrup is completely clear, increase the heat and cook to a light caramel, about 5 minutes.

2 Remove from the heat and carefully stir in the orange juice; it will splutter. Slit open the vanilla pod, scrape out the seeds and add these to the caramel sauce. Set aside to cool until thickened.

3 Preheat the oven to 150°C, Gas 2. Brush the peaches liberally with the butter using a pastry brush, then sprinkle with the remaining sugar and roll them to coat thoroughly.

4 Place the peaches in a small roasting tin and spoon the caramel over them. Roast, uncovered, in the oven for about 30 minutes until the peaches are softened but still whole, basting them with the pan juices every 10 minutes or so.

5 Cover loosely with a 'tent' of foil and leave to cool; this encourages juices to gather in the bottom of the tin.

6 Peel off any loose skin, but don't strip the peaches completely – they look good with some skin still attached. Stir up the pan juices, strain through a sieve and set aside in a jug.

7 Serve the peaches lightly chilled, with the orange caramel sauce spooned over. I like to top the peaches with sugar-crusted basil leaves.

DELICIOUS SERVED WITH WHITE PEACH PARFAIT (PAGE 71)

Baked apples with peppercorns

Here you need to use a variety of apple that holds its shape and texture well on baking – such as Granny Smith or Braeburn. After the initial caramelising, the apples are flavoured with crushed peppercorns and vanilla and baked in the oven until tender. I find that peppercorns really enhance the flavour of sweet things – especially fruits.

1 Peel the apples neatly using a small paring knife, and scoop out the cores with an apple corer. Pat dry with kitchen paper, then brush all over with the softened butter. Roll in the demerara sugar to coat.

2 Preheat the oven to 190°C, Gas 5. Place the apples in a roasting tin or baking dish and roast in the oven for 10 minutes.

3 Pour in the apple juice and scatter over the crushed peppercorns and vanilla pod. Spoon the juice over the apples, then return to the oven. Roast, uncovered, for a further 20 minutes, basting the fruits every 5 minutes or so. On the final basting, trickle over the Armagnac, if using.

4 Allow to cool for 10 minutes or longer, basting the apples occasionally with the pan juices.

5 To serve, lift the apples into a serving dish and strain the pan juices over. For a simple dessert, serve warm with pouring cream or Crème anglaise (page 193) and Cumin or Hazelnut shortbreads (page 172).

SERVES 6

6 firm dessert apples, such as Granny Smith or Braeburn

about 100g butter, softened until runny but not melted

about 100g unrefined demerara sugar

300ml apple juice

1 teaspoon crushed black peppercorns

1 teaspoon crushed dried pink peppercorns

1 vanilla pod, slit open

2–3 tablespoons Armagnac (optional)

THESE APPLES ARE ESPECIALLY GOOD SERVED WARM WITH A CREAMY BAVAROIS (PAGES 97–7) OR PARFAIT (PAGES 64–71)

Baby roasted pineapples

SERVES 4

4 baby pineapples, or 1 medium sweet
    pineapple
about 16–28 whole cloves
250g caster sugar
460ml water
1 teaspoon Chinese five-spice powder
1 cinnamon stick

When you come across baby pineapples, buy some and bake them to a funky rasta look. Check their ripeness by pulling a green leaf at the top – it should come out quite easily. You'll need to make up a caramel syrup a day in advance then macerate the peeled fruits overnight. The next day, simply open-roast the whole fruit, basting occasionally with the spiced syrup. You can do the same with a larger pineapple, slicing it first.

1 If using baby pineapples, peel the skin but leave on the tops and dig out the 'eyes' with the tip of a knife. If using a larger pineapple, cut off the top, peel and remove the 'eyes', then slice. Push the cloves into the 'eye sockets'.

2 Now, make the syrup. Put the sugar and 4 tablespoons of water in a heavy-based saucepan and dissolve very slowly over a gentle heat – you may need to swirl the pan occasionally, but avoid stirring. When the syrup is clear and no sugar grains remain, raise the heat and boil for about 7 minutes to a light caramel colour.

3 Remove from the heat and carefully stir in 400ml water – standing back as it will spit. Stir in the spices.

4 Place the fruit in a large heavy-based saucepan and pour over the caramel syrup. Heat gently for about 5 minutes, basting with the syrup. Transfer the fruit to a bowl, pour over the syrup and set aside to cool, stirring once or twice. Cover and leave to macerate overnight.

5 The next day, preheat the oven to 190°C, Gas 5. Place the fruits in a small roasting tin or baking dish and spoon over some of the syrup. Roast for 15–20 minutes, basting two or three times with the syrup. The fruit should soften but still hold a good shape. Leave to cool to room temperature.

6 Serve the pineapples with some of the spiced syrup spooned over.

SUBLIME WITH PINEAPPLE AND STAR ANISE MOUSSE (PAGE 87), OR A CREAMY PARFAIT SUCH AS WHITE PEACH PARFAIT (PAGE 71)

Roasted plums

Try roasting plums instead of poaching them in syrup. They take on a more inviting caramelised flavour – wonderful with any of the creamy mousses and bavarois (pages 86–97), and parfaits (pages 64–71). You could also turn your hand to the classic French Tête à brioche (below and illustrated) with their hidden nuggets of fruit.

1 Halve and stone the plums, then cut into quarters. Place in a single layer in a shallow ovenproof dish. Preheat the oven to 190°C, Gas 5.
2 Put the butter and sugar in a small pan with the vanilla pod and cinnamon stick, and heat gently until melted. Trickle the buttery syrup over the plums, stirring gently to coat.
3 Roast uncovered for about 10–15 minutes, basting two or three times with the pan juices. Allow to cool, then discard the vanilla pod and cinnamon stick.
4 For a simple dessert, serve with Orange and cardamom cream (page 55), Prune and armagnac ice cream (page 63) or Ginger ice cream (page 58) and, perhaps, some Shortbreads (page 172).

Tête à brioche

1 Prepare the roasted plums (as above), or soak 6 plump mi-cuit Agen prunes in water to cover until softened. Drain the fruit. Stone the prunes if necessary.
2 Make a slightly firmer dough than the basic Brioche loaf recipe (page 210), by using 4 medium eggs instead of six. Brush the insides of 12 muffin tins or fluted baby brioche tins with melted butter. After the first rising, knock back the dough and set aside a quarter of it.
3 Divide the larger portion of dough into 12 pieces, shape into balls and drop into the tins. With your thumb, press a deep hole in the centre of each brioche bun and place a roasted plum quarter or soaked prune in the hole. Shape the remaining dough into 12 smaller balls and position on top. Leave to prove in a warm place until almost doubled in size.
4 Bake at 190°C, Gas 5 for 15–20 minutes until golden brown and firm. Leave in the tins for 5 minutes then loosen the buns with the tip of a knife and turn out on to a wire rack to cool. Perfect for a special brunch.

SERVES 4
8 large red plums
50g butter
50g caster sugar
1 vanilla pod, slit open
1 cinnamon stick

TETE A BRIOCHE ARE AN ORIGINAL WAY OF PRESENTING ROASTED PLUMS AND PRUNES

Roasted black figs with spiced balsamic syrup

SERVES 6

6 large black Mission figs

3 tablespoons Acacia or pine-scented clear honey

150ml Stock syrup (page 200)

2 cinnamon sticks

2 cloves

2 vanilla pods, slit open

3 star anise

strips of zest from 1 orange

3 tablespoons aged balsamic vinegar

SERVE WITH A SPICY ICE CREAM, SUCH AS CARDAMOM OR GINGER (PAGE 58)

Make this simple recipe when you find large black Mission figs in the shops during late summer. The aromatic syrup can be strained after baking and used again.

1 Trim the tips off the fig stalks and stand the figs in a medium shallow roasting tin. Preheat the oven to 150°C, Gas 2.

2 Meanwhile, put all the remaining ingredients into a heavy-based saucepan, bring to the boil and boil until reduced to a syrupy glaze, about 3 minutes.

3 Spoon the syrup over the figs. Bake uncovered for about 30 minutes, basting every 10 minutes or so, until the figs are soft when pierced with a skewer, but still holding their shape.

4 Serve the figs warm, with a little syrup spooned over. Strain the rest of the sauce into a screw-topped jar and refrigerate for another time.

Honey roasted green figs

Use green figs and omit the cinnamon, cloves, star anise and balsamic vinegar for a more subtle honey-flavoured syrup.

Caramelised mango slices

SERVES 4

2 large, just ripe mangoes

20g butter

1 tablespoon caster sugar

3 tablespoons icing sugar

2 good pinches of Chinese five-spice powder

FOR A SIMPLE DESSERT, ACCOMPANY WITH RASPBERRY CREAM (PAGE 51) OR PISTACHIO CREAM (PAGE 52)

These are superb with creamy ices and mousses, especially Mango and passion fruit parfait (page 69) and Mango and dark chocolate mousse (page 88). Conveniently, they can be cooked ahead and then reheated.

1 Cut the mangoes either side of the flat stone, then peel and slice the flesh. Place in a shallow dish.

2 Put the butter and caster sugar in a heavy-based frying pan and heat gently, stirring, until melted. Increase the heat and cook until the buttery syrup is a light caramel colour.

3 Meanwhile, sift the icing sugar and spice together over the mangoes. Toss the fruit to coat.

4 Add the mango slices to the hot pan in a single layer and cook for about 5 minutes, turning once, until lightly browned on both sides. Leave to cool slightly in the pan juices. Serve warm.

Slow roasted pears

These are delicious served lightly chilled with a flavoured crème fraîche (page 50) or as an accompaniment to one of my creamy mousses or bavarois (pages 86–97), or parfaits (pages 64–71). Choose well-rounded pears such as Williams or Comice that will sit nicely balanced on a plate.

1 Peel the pears, leaving them whole. Using a small sharp knife, scoop out as much of the core from the base as possible, then cut off a thin slice to make sure the pears will stand upright. Brush them all over with some of the lime juice and leave to stand for about 5 minutes.
2 Meanwhile, preheat the oven to 190°C, Gas 5. Tip the sugar into a shallow bowl.
3 Pat the pears lightly with kitchen paper to dry, then brush them all over with the softened butter and roll in the sugar to coat.
4 Stand the pears upright in a shallow baking dish and roast for about 15 minutes until they start to colour.
5 Meanwhile, mix the remaining lime juice with the grated zest, leftover sugar and eau-de-vie. Spoon over the pears and add the vanilla pod. Bake for a further 15 minutes, basting with the pan juices at least twice. Test the pears with a fine skewer or thin-bladed knife – they should feel tender but still hold their shape. Remove and cool, brushing occasionally with the juices.

SERVES 6
6 even-sized medium firm pears
grated zest and juice of 3 limes
100g butter, softened until runny but not melted
100g caster or light soft brown sugar
2 tablespoons poire eau-de-vie
1 vanilla pod, slit open

Glazed apricots

In the restaurant, we serve these with Rum babas (page 119), but they are equally good with Thai rice pudding (page 132) or served simply with ice cream and shortbread biscuits.

1 Halve the apricots and remove the stones. Place in a single layer in a shallow dish. Dredge with the sugar, then sprinkle over the rum or Amaretto. Leave for an hour, mixing gently once or twice.
2 Now, heat a large heavy-based frying pan over a medium heat until you can feel a strong heat rising. Carefully lay the apricots in the pan, cut-side down, and cook until they start to caramelise.
3 Gently flip the fruit over with a palette knife and cook the other side until caramelised. Don't move them about too much in the pan or they will break up and not caramelise properly. Remove from the heat and allow to cool slightly. Best served slightly warm.

SERVES 4–6
12 just ripe apricots
125g caster sugar
3 tablespoons rum or Amaretto liqueur

DRYING FRUIT SLICES

I am a great believer in flaunting beauty and fresh fruits are designed to be paraded stripped to their bare shapes. One of the simplest and most stunning decorations is wafer-thin slices of firm fruit that have been dried in a warm oven until almost translucent and crisp (illustrated on pages 44–5). All fruits are prepared in the same way, except that those susceptible to discoloration are best treated with lemon juice (see below) as soon as they are sliced.

I enjoy experimenting with new fruits. In the restaurant we currently favour apples, pears, strawberries, pineapples, kiwis, figs, mango and peaches. The fruit is best sliced just before it is ripe so the colour is bright and the flesh is firm, but not too juicy. Needless to say you need to use perfect, unblemished fruits.

To prepare dried fruit slices

1 First, make up a quantity of simple Stock syrup (page 200).
2 Turn the oven on to its lowest setting – probably indicated as slow or warm on your oven dial. Line 2 baking sheets with a silicone cooking liner (such as silpat or bake-o-glide). I find baking parchment isn't sufficiently non-stick for this purpose and becomes wet.
3 Prepare your chosen fruit. Only pineapples and mangoes should be peeled. Use a sharp serrated fruit knife to cut the fruit into wafer-thin slices. (We use the bacon slicer in our kitchen, but I can't imagine you have one!) Don't halve and stone fruit such as peaches, plums, mangoes etc. Instead, slice until you reach the stone then turn the fruit around and slice the other side. Apples and pears are best cored neatly, although pears can be sliced whole lengthways up to the core. Dip apples, pears and other fruits that are prone to discoloration into a little sugar syrup mixed with a squeeze of lemon juice as soon as you slice them.
4 Dip the fruit slices quickly into the stock syrup, shake off excess syrup and lay them out in neat rows on the silicone cooking liners. Leave in the low oven for a good 2 hours. If the fruit appears to be starting to brown, the oven is too warm. To lower the temperature, try propping open the door with the handle of a wooden spoon.
5 The slices are ready when they feel firm and can be lifted off easily. Don't leave them in the oven for longer than is necessary. They crisp up on cooling.
6 Store the dried fruit slices in airtight plastic containers. If properly dried, they will keep crisp for at least a week.

CITRUS FRUIT CONFIT

These make another elegant finishing touch and you can prepare them well ahead. A jar of citrus confit slices makes an attractive foodie gift. Either prepare a single variety or a mixture of citrus fruits – lemon and lime is a useful combination. Use organic unwaxed fruit if possible.

To prepare citrus fruit confit slices

1 Wash 2 large seedless oranges, 3 lemons or 3 limes (or a combination of these), but do not peel the fruit. Pat dry, then cut into thin slices, about 3mm thick.

2 Make up a batch of Stock syrup (page 200) – 250ml should be enough. Bring it back to the boil and drop in the fruit slices. Remove from the heat and leave to cool.

3 Spoon the fruit and syrup into a screw-topped jar and store in the fridge. Remove the confit slices to use when required. They can be kept in the fridge for up to 1 month.

4 When all the confit slices are gone, you can re-boil the syrup (which will be citrus-scented) then strain and use it again.

Variation

To make kumquat confit, wash about 250g kumquats and pat dry on kitchen paper. Cut the tiny citrus fruit in half crossways. Add to 250ml boiling Stock syrup (as above), then immediately take off the heat and cool. Finish as above.

To prepare citrus zest confit strips

1 Wash 2 large seedless oranges, 3 lemons or 3 limes (or a combination of these), and pat dry. Finely pare the zest using a swivel vegetable peeler. Scrape off any pith, then cut the zest into thin julienne strips.

2 Blanch the citrus zest in boiling water for 2 minutes, then drain and pat dry.

3 Bring 250ml Stock syrup (page 200) to the boil in a small pan. Drop the citrus zest into the pan, bring back to the boil and simmer for about 3 minutes. Remove from the heat and leave to cool.

4 Spoon the zest strips and syrup into a screw-topped jar and store in the fridge for up to 1 month. Remove the zest to use when required.

SERVE CITRUS CONFITS AS A DECORATIVE FINISHING TOUCH ON THE SIDE. THEY COMPLEMENT LEMON AND PASSION FRUIT TARTLETS (PAGE 155), TREACLE TART (PAGE 138) AND BANANAS IN CARAMEL RUM SYRUP (PAGE 24) PARTICULARLY WELL

ices and creams

FLAVOURED CREAMS

These have a number of uses. You can serve them with fresh fruit salads, tarts, roasted fruits and hot puddings, or spoon them into little tartlet cases, brandy snaps, or my Filo horns (page 152). Serving quantities depend on the end use. Creams look most attractive shaped into quenelles.

To shape oval quenelles
1 First, cover a plate tightly with cling film, so that it is stretched across the rim and held above the surface of the plate. Make sure the cream is well packed in the bowl, tapping firmly on the work surface to exclude air bubbles. Dip a dessertspoon into a bowl of hot water to warm it, dry on a tea towel, then dip sideways into the cream and curl the spoon to take up an oval quenelle.
2 Neaten the edge against the side of the bowl, then rub the base of the spoon in the palm of your hand to warm it slightly.
3 Tip the quenelle out sideways on to the cling film. Repeat to make as many as you need, then chill until required. Mousses, ice creams and sorbets can also be shaped into quenelles.

Note: For a shiny finish, leave the inside of the spoon wet after dipping it into the hot water. The moisture will glaze the quenelle.

Crème chantilly

The most basic of creams, this is simply lightly sweetened whipped cream. It should have the consistency of soft meringue with floppy peaks. To avoid over-whipping I suggest you add 2 tablespoons milk to each 300ml cream, with 1–2 tablespoons caster sugar, before beating. For best results, chill the bowl and beaters and, of course, make sure your cream is very fresh and chilled. Stand the bowl on a damp cloth to hold it steady. We whip our cream by machine but the speed must be very low as the cream begins to thicken – it can 'turn' quite suddenly. Also, cream thickens on standing, so don't beat too far in advance – about 10 minutes is fine.

Flavoured crème fraîche

Full-fat crème fraîche can be whipped and flavoured with infused Stock syrup (page 10), allowing 2 tablespoons for every 200ml cream. Use syrup infused with lemon grass, vanilla or spices. Lemon grass crème fraîche is delicious with treacle tart; spiced crème fraîche complements mince pies and Christmas pudding. Or try whipping crème fraîche with some of the syrup from a jar of stem ginger and serve with hot roasted fruits.

Raspberry cream

Serve as little dessert tasters in elegant liqueur glasses topped with some dainty berry fruits – like a pink syllabub. Alternatively layer with sugar-dusted layers of puff pastry mille-feuille style, or pipe into filo horns. To make the cream fruitier, fold in some crushed raspberries or loganberries, when in season.

1 Purée the raspberries in a food processor or blender to a pulp. Add the lemon juice and sweeten with icing sugar if required. Pass the purée through a sieve into a bowl, rubbing it through with the back of a ladle. Cover and chill.

2 Just before serving, whip the cream until it forms soft, floppy peaks, then fold in the raspberry purée. The mixture will immediately thicken up (which is why you should combine it at the last moment).

SERVES 6–8
200g raspberries
squeeze of lemon juice
1–2 tablespoons icing sugar, sifted (optional)
300ml double cream, chilled

Passion fruit cream

The passion fruit concentrate we use in the restaurant is difficult to buy, so you will need to make your own for this fragrant cream, using the juice from plenty of fruit and boiling to concentrate the flavour. Buy passion fruit that are shrivelled and look beyond hope – in fact they will be at their best and full of juicy flavour. Sometimes you see fresh orange juice flavoured with passion fruit juice – you could boil this down instead for a similar flavour.

1 Halve the passion fruit and scoop out the pulp and seeds into a food processor or blender. Whiz thoroughly, scraping down the sides frequently. This releases the pectin in the seeds, which helps to thicken the cream.

2 Now, boil the passion fruit purée in a small pan until reduced by half; this takes about 5 minutes. Rub through a sieve into a bowl with the back of a small ladle or wooden spoon. Cool, then cover and chill.

3 Mix the passion juice into the mascarpone. In another bowl, whip the cream with the icing sugar until it forms soft peaks and then fold into the passion fruit mixture. Chill lightly before serving.

SERVES 6–8
8 ripe passion fruit
150g mascarpone
150ml whipping cream
2–3 tablespoons icing sugar

SERVE FRUIT CREAMS IN SMALL STEMMED GLASSES WITH LANGUES DE CHAT (PAGE 173) OR OTHER DESSERT BISCUITS, OR PIPE INTO FILO HORNS (PAGE 152)

Pistachio cream

SERVES 4–6
125g shelled unsalted pistachios
3 tablespoons Stock syrup (page 200)
300ml double cream

ROASTED FRUITS SUCH AS CARAMELISED
MANGO SLICES (PAGE 42) ARE DELICIOUS
TOPPED WITH A DOLLOP OF PISTACHIO
CREAM, AS ILLUSTRATED

We use pistachio paste to make this cream in the restaurant, but it isn't available to the home cook. However, you can make a good substitute by grinding pistachios in a coffee grinder then blending with stock syrup.

1 First, wipe the coffee grinder clean of all traces of coffee, using a wad of kitchen paper or a dry, clean dishcloth. Finely grind the nuts in 2 or 3 batches until they are almost reduced to a paste.
2 Tip the nuts into a food processor or blender and whiz with the stock syrup until evenly blended. (Don't try to do this in a coffee grinder – most aren't liquid proof.)
3 Whip the cream in a bowl until it forms soft floppy peaks. Fold in the pistachio paste. Chill lightly before serving.

Roasted almond cream

SERVES 6
75g blanched almonds, very finely chopped
15g icing sugar, sifted
300ml double cream
2 tablespoons ground almonds
2 tablespoons Amaretto liqueur

A rich, nutty cream to complement roasted fruits, especially pears, plums and peaches. Also good with Caramelised pear tatin (page 142).

1 Heat the chopped almonds in a large heavy-based frying pan, stirring occasionally until they start to turn golden brown.
2 Sprinkle over the icing sugar. As it begins to caramelise it will give out a wonderful aroma. Remove from the heat before the sugar turns too dark, then tip on to a plate to cool completely. Stir the sugar-dusted nuts frequently as they cool to keep them free-flowing.
3 Now, whip the cream in a bowl until it forms soft floppy peaks. Fold in the ground almonds, liqueur, and finally the cold roasted sugar nuts. Chill lightly before serving.

Lemon and lime cream

SERVES 4–6
finely grated zest and juice of 2 large lemons
finely grated zest and juice of 3 limes
40g caster sugar
125g mascarpone
150ml double cream

1 Mix the lemon and lime zests with the sugar. Bring the citrus juices to the boil in a small pan and boil until reduced to about 2 tablespoons. Mix with the zesty sugar and cool.
2 Beat the citrus sugar mixture into the mascarpone.
3 Whip the cream until it forms soft floppy peaks and fold into the fruity mascarpone. Serve lightly chilled.

Mascarpone and vanilla hearts

This is an update of the classic French cœur à la crème dessert. You will need six porcelain perforated heart-shaped moulds and wet muslin to line them. Most good cook's shops stock these items or supply them by mail order. The luscious mixture of three creams is left to drain overnight, to become even richer and more delicious. Serve simply with fresh soft fruits and nutty shortbreads – half-dipped in melted dark chocolate if you like.

1 Beat the mascarpone and cream cheese together in a bowl until smooth. Slit the vanilla pod lengthways and scrape out the seeds with the tip of a knife. Add these to the mascarpone mixture with the sugar and beat well.
2 Whip the crème fraîche in another bowl until softly stiff and fold into the mixture.
3 Line 6 cœur de crème moulds with wet muslin allowing some overhang. Spoon in the vanilla cream and level with a palette knife. Chill for at least 24 hours.
4 Unmould the vanilla creams on to serving plates and peel off the muslin. Serve with a selection of soft summer fruits and crisp biscuits.

SERVES 6
200g mascarpone
100g cream cheese
1 vanilla pod
150g caster sugar
150g crème fraîche
soft fruits, such as strawberries, raspberries, red or white currants, to serve

HAZELNUT SHORTBREADS (PAGE 172) ARE THE IDEAL FOIL FOR THESE SMOOTH, VELVETY CREAMS

Orange and cardamom cream

An aromatic cream ideal for spooning over hot winter fruit puddings – especially a good homemade Christmas pudding or buttery mince pies. For a stronger flavour, bruise the cardamom pods before adding them.

1 Grate the zest from 1 orange and the lemon. Squeeze the juice from all of the fruits. Put the citrus zests and juices in a small pan with the cardamom pods and sugar. Bring to the boil and boil until reduced by half. Allow to cool.
2 Pass the cooled citrus liquid through a sieve into a small bowl, rubbing it through with the back of a spoon. Discard the cardamoms.
3 Beat the cream in a bowl until it forms soft floppy peaks and then fold in the citrus juice and liqueur. Chill before serving.

SERVES 6
2 large oranges
1 lemon
4 cardamom pods
2 tablespoons caster sugar
300ml double cream
1 tablespoon Grand Marnier or Cointreau

ICE CREAMS

We always have a good variety of rich ice creams in our restaurant freezers, as they complement so many of my desserts. The base for most good homemade ice creams is crème anglaise, although some of my ices rely on pâte à bombe instead. The key to success is a smooth texture and churning the chilled mixture in an ice cream machine is the best way to achieve this. To churn successfully you need sufficient mixture – the quantities suggested here for Classic vanilla ice cream (right) are twice the basic crème anglaise recipe (on page 193) and work well. Once the mixture is creamy and almost frozen firm, you can transfer it to a suitable container and pop it in the freezer.

If you do not have an ice cream maker, the mixture can be frozen in a shallow container but you must beat it thoroughly at least three times during freezing. The more you beat a semi-frozen mixture, the smaller the ice crystals become and the smoother the end result.

Ice cream readily absorbs the flavours of other food stored alongside it, so make sure containers are well sealed. For the freshest flavour, homemade ice cream is best eaten soon after churning, or at least within a week. Unless you serve the ice cream soon after freezing, you will need to soften it at room temperature for about 10 minutes before scooping.

Classic vanilla ice cream

You can always tell a real vanilla ice cream – it will be pale yellow and speckled with tiny black seeds.

1 Make the crème anglaise (according to the method on page 193). Cool quickly over a bowl of iced water and chill thoroughly.

2 Pour the chilled crème anglaise into an ice cream machine and churn.

3 When the ice cream is almost firm, you can transfer it to a freezer container, seal well and put into the freezer unless, of course, you are serving it at once. If you do not have an ice cream machine, freeze the mixture in a shallow container, beating during freezing (see left).

4 For optimum flavour, eat within 1 week, remembering to soften the ice cream at room temperature for about 10 minutes before serving.

MAKES ABOUT 1.2 LITRES

CRÈME ANGLAISE:

500ml whole milk

500ml double cream

100g caster sugar

12 large free-range egg yolks

2–3 vanilla pods

Variations of vanilla ice cream

CARDAMOM ICE CREAM This is sensational. Make as for Classic vanilla ice cream (page 57), omitting the vanilla from the crème anglaise. Instead, steep 1 tablespoon green cardamom pods in the milk and cream.

Alternatively, for a stronger flavour, crack open 6–8 cardamom pods, extract the tiny black seeds and add these to the milk and cream with the empty pods. Strain the flavoured crème anglaise after, rather than before chilling.

GINGER ICE CREAM An ice cream for ginger freaks – those who could happily eat a whole jar of stem ginger at Christmas! Make as for Classic vanilla ice cream (page 57), omitting the vanilla from the crème anglaise. Instead, peel and grate a 3cm cube of fresh root ginger and steep in the creamy milk. For extra flavour, stir 2 finely chopped pieces of preserved stem ginger (drained of syrup) into the cooled custard.

RUM AND RAISIN ICE CREAM Churn Classic vanilla (page 57) or Cardamom ice cream (above) until slushy. Add 6–8 spoonfuls of Macerated fruits (page 13) and continue churning until firm. Or simply stir the fruits into softened ice cream.

BAILEYS ICE CREAM Add 200ml Baileys liqueur to the Classic vanilla ice cream (page 57) before churning. Serve in scoops with more Baileys drizzled over.

FRESH LAVENDER ICE CREAM You need fresh flowers for this fragrant ice cream, which are around in late summer. Make as for Classic vanilla ice cream (page 57), omitting the vanilla from the crème anglaise. Instead, strip the flower buds from about 50g of fresh lavender flowers and steep these in the hot cream and milk. Strain after, rather than before chilling.

STRAWBERRY ICE CREAM Make a single quantity of Crème anglaise (page 193) and chill. Hull 500g ripe strawberries and purée in a food processor or blender. Transfer to a fairly deep heavy-based saucepan and boil until reduced by half. This takes about 12–15 minutes and helps to concentrate the flavour. Cool. Strain to remove the seeds, if preferred. Beat the strawberry purée into the chilled crème anglaise and continue as for Classic vanilla ice cream (page 57).

CHOCOLATE CHIP ICE CREAM Churn a quantity of Classic vanilla ice cream (page 57) until slushy. Finely chop 150g dark chocolate, add to the ice cream and continue churning until firm.

Orange flower water ice cream

We don't make enough use of concentrated flower waters, which is a pity as a few drops can transform a simple recipe into something memorable – like this ice cream. We serve it in dainty scoops on orange jellies, but it would go marvellously with strawberries, raspberries or even scooped on top of hot apple pie or treacle tart. Orange flower water is available from the baking section of selected supermarkets and delis.

1 Put the cream and milk in a heavy-based saucepan with 1 tablespoon of the sugar and slowly bring to the boil.

2 Meanwhile, whisk the remaining sugar and egg yolks together in a large bowl using an electric beater until pale golden and fluffy.

3 As soon as the creamy milk starts to rise up the side of the pan, take off the heat and pour a third of it in small slurps on to the sugary egg yolks, whisking as you pour.

4 Pour back into the saucepan and cook, stirring constantly, on a very low heat until the custard coats the back of a wooden spoon, like thick cream. Alternatively, you can use a sugar thermometer to check when it is ready – the temperature should read 82°C.

5 Strain the custard through a fine sieve into a bowl and leave to cool, stirring occasionally to prevent a skin forming.

6 When cold, add a few drops of orange flower water and taste. Does it need more? If so, add one or two extra drops – remember mixtures need more flavouring if they are eaten frozen.

7 Churn in an ice cream machine until almost firm, then transfer to a freezer container, seal and put into the freezer. If you do not have an ice cream machine, freeze in a shallow container, beating during freezing (see page 56).

8 For optimum flavour, eat soon after making – at most within 1 week. Allow to soften at room temperature for 10–15 minutes before scooping. We freeze small scoops of this ice cream on non-stick silicone sheets so they can be served quickly.

MAKES ABOUT 600ml
250ml double cream
250ml whole milk
75g caster sugar
5 large free-range egg yolks
few drops of orange flower water, to taste

SERVE IN DAINTY SCOOPS ON BLOOD ORANGE JELLIES (PAGE 32) WITH A TRICKLE OF PASSION FRUIT COULIS (PAGE 11) AND A FINANCIER (PAGE 173) ON THE SIDE

Chocolate and thyme ice cream

Pâte à bombe gives this unusual ice cream a wonderful light texture whilst the thyme imparts an intriguing flavour. Good quality dark chocolate is essential.

1 Make the pâte à bombe and set aside.
2 Put the milk and sugar in a saucepan and slowly bring to the boil. Remove from the heat, add the thyme sprigs and set aside to infuse for 20 minutes. Strain through a sieve to remove the thyme.
3 Meanwhile, break up the chocolate and place in a large heatproof bowl. Heat the cream until almost boiling, then slowly pour on to the chocolate, stirring well until melted. Whisk in the infused milk and allow to cool to room temperature.
4 Fold the pâte à bombe into the cooled chocolate mixture. Churn and freeze as for Classic vanilla ice cream (page 57).

MAKES ABOUT 1.2 LITRES
1 quantity Pâte à bombe (page 198)
250ml whole milk
50g caster sugar
about 4–5 large fresh thyme sprigs
200g dark chocolate (at least 60% cocoa solids)
250ml double cream

SERVE ON ITS OWN OR WITH A SELECTION OF OTHER ICES SUCH AS VANILLA (PAGE 57), PRUNE AND ARMAGNAC (PAGE 63) AND CHOCOLATE CHIP (PAGE 58), AS SHOWN

Angelica ice cream

If you have angelica growing in your garden, then do try this original ice cream. (It grows prolifically and is available from garden centres.) We associate angelica with tutti fruiti ices and cake decorations, but its history is more illustrious. Did you know, for example, that this ancient herb is the main flavouring for green Chartreuse?

1 Make the pâte à bombe and set aside.
2 Put the milk and cream into a saucepan, add the chopped angelica stalks and sugar and bring slowly to the boil. Take off the heat and set aside to infuse for 20–30 minutes. Strain through a sieve and discard the angelica. Allow to cool.
3 Mix the pâte à bombe with the infused creamy milk. If adding candied angelica, rinse to remove the sugar, pat dry and chop finely.
4 Churn the mixture as for Classic vanilla ice cream (page 57) adding the candied angelica, if using, when the ice cream is slushy. Continue to churn until almost firm and freeze as for vanilla ice cream.

Note: *If fresh angelica isn't available infuse the creamy milk with 100g candied angelica instead.*

MAKES ABOUT 1.2 LITRES
1 quantity Pâte à bombe (page 198)
250ml whole milk
250ml double cream
50g fresh angelica stalks. chopped (see note)
50g caster sugar
25g candied angelica (optional)

ANGELICA ICE CREAM IS NICE WITH SLICED FRESH PINEAPPLE AND KIWI FRUIT

Liquorice ice cream

MAKES ABOUT 600ml

350ml whole milk

120ml double cream

2 small liquorice sticks, or 50g liquorice
    pastilles

8 large free-range egg yolks

40g light muscovado sugar

40g caster sugar

There is renewed interest in liquorice as a flavouring now that you can buy dried liquorice twigs from healthfood shops and it makes fabulous desserts. This ice cream may not be the most appealing colour, but it still tastes good. If you can't find liquorice twigs, you can use black liquorice pastilles or Pontefract cakes instead.

1 Put the milk, cream and liquorice sticks or pastilles in a heavy-based saucepan and slowly bring to the boil. If using pastilles, stir until the liquorice has dissolved. If using liquorice sticks, allow to infuse off the heat for 30 minutes.

2 Meanwhile, beat the egg yolks and both sugars together in a bowl until thick and creamy. Return the creamy flavoured milk to the boil, then gradually pour a third of it on to the sugar and yolks in cautious slurps, beating well.

3 Strain the mixture back into the saucepan and stir over the lowest heat possible until the custard starts to thicken slightly, about 5–7 minutes. Don't allow to come to the boil or it will curdle. When you can draw a line down the back of the wooden spoon with your finger and it leaves an impression, the custard is ready.

4 Pour the custard into a chilled bowl and cool, stirring occasionally to prevent a skin forming. Chill.

5 Churn and freeze as for Classic vanilla ice cream (page 57). Allow to soften at room temperature for 10–15 minutes before scooping into balls, or scrape off shavings with a large metal spoon.

Prune and armagnac ice cream

These prunes have a variety of other uses, so I suggest you make a double quantity – store in a large screw-topped jar in the fridge. Spoon them over hot rice pudding, or ready-made ice cream to give it a kick.

1 To prepare the prunes, stone and chop them into pieces the size of large raisins. Place in a saucepan with the Armagnac, sugar and water. Slit the vanilla pod lengthways and scrape out the seeds with the tip of a sharp knife, adding them to the pan; reserve the pod.
2 Slowly bring to the boil, then take off the heat and leave to steep for 24 hours before decanting into a screw-topped jar. Chill until required.
3 For the ice cream, make the pâte à bombe and set aside. Put the milk and cream in a saucepan, add the reserved vanilla pod and bring to the boil. Take off the heat and set aside to infuse until cold. Discard the vanilla pod, then whisk the creamy milk into the pâte à bombe. Chill.
4 Churn as for Classic vanilla ice cream (page 57), adding the macerated prunes and liquor when the mixture is creamy and slushy. Continue to churn until firm and freeze as for vanilla ice cream.

MAKES ABOUT 1.2 LITRES
MACERATED PRUNES:
125g mi-cuit (no-need-to-soak) Agen prunes
125ml Armagnac
3 tablespoons caster sugar
2 tablespoons water
1 vanilla pod
ICE CREAM:
1 quantity Pâte à bombe (page 198)
120ml whole milk
120ml double cream

THIS DELICIOUSLY RICH ICE CREAM GOES BRILLIANTLY WITH CHRISTMAS PUDDING AND MINCE PIES

Banana ice cream

Homemade banana ice cream is quite fabulous, especially served with hot fruit salads, crumbles and apple pies. For the best flavour use bananas that are very spotty and slightly soft.

1 Put the cream, milk, salt and 2 tablespoons of the sugar in a large non-stick saucepan over a low heat. Finely chop the bananas and add to the pan. Bring to the boil and simmer gently for 10–15 minutes. Mash the bananas as they cook against the side of the pan.
2 Meanwhile, beat the remaining sugar and egg yolks in a large heatproof bowl until thick and creamy.
3 Strain the creamy milk through a sieve into a jug, then pour on to the yolk mixture, whisking well. Return to the pan and cook on a very low heat, stirring with a wooden spoon, until slightly thickened. This takes 5–10 minutes. Don't let the mixture even start to boil or it will curdle. To test, draw a line down the back of the wooden spoon – if it leaves an impression, the custard is ready. Strain into a bowl.
4 Cool, stirring frequently to stop a skin forming, then cover and chill. Churn and freeze as for Classic vanilla ice cream (page 57).

MAKES ABOUT 1 LITRE
300ml double cream
350ml whole milk
1/4 teaspoon sea salt
130g caster sugar
4 large ripe bananas
5 large free-range egg yolks

THIS RICH, CREAMY ICE IS EXCELLENT SERVED WITH BANANAS IN CARAMEL RUM SYRUP (PAGE 24)

PARFAITS

Parfaits are the ultimate make-ahead iced dessert – perfect for entertaining. They can be frozen well in advance – in individual or large moulds – and served within minutes of taking from the freezer. If frozen whole in terrines or loaf tins, unmould the parfait while it is still frozen and cut into slices to serve. In the restaurant we use all sorts of chic shaped moulds for individual parfaits, such as pyramids and cubes, but good old-fashioned dariole moulds look just as good. (You could even use little yogurt pots.) Once frozen, parfaits can be turned out then wrapped well in freezer film and stored in the freezer for up to 1 month. Allow larger parfaits to soften at room temperature for 5–10 minutes before slicing to serve.

Note: Some of these parfaits contain raw egg white and should be avoided by those who are particularly at risk from salmonella.

Strawberry and vanilla semi-freddo

SERVES 6–8
1 quantity Pâte à bombe (page 198)
250g strawberries, hulled
125g redcurrants, stripped from their stalks
200ml double cream
1 vanilla pod

This is a very simple parfait – fresh fruit purée mixed with pâte à bombe and whipped cream. Make it when homegrown strawberries are at their peak – full of flavour and colour, vital qualities for frozen desserts. Ideally, serve the parfait sliced with some wild strawberries or assorted summer berries and trickles of fruit coulis.

1 Make the pâte à bombe. Purée the strawberries and redcurrants in a food processor or blender until smooth, then sieve to remove the seeds if preferred. Fold the purée into the pâte à bombe. Cover and chill the mixture for 1 hour.
2 Pour the cream into a bowl. Slit open the vanilla pod and scrape out the seeds with the tip of a knife, adding these to the cream. Three-quarters whip the cream until softly peaking.
3 Fold the vanilla cream into the strawberry mixture, then freeze in a 1.2 litre loaf tin or individual moulds.
4 To unmould a large parfait, dip the mould into warm water for a few seconds, then invert on to a board and soften at room temperature for 5–10 minutes before slicing. Turn out individual parfaits straight on to serving plates.

APPEALING WITH A SIDE DECORATION OF SUMMER BERRIES AND TRICKLES OF BLACKCURRANT COULIS (PAGE 12)

Nougat parfait

Nougat is associated with the French town of Montelimar and has been a Mediterranean favourite for centuries. Basically it is a chewy sweet of boiled honey, sugar and egg white mixed with glacé fruits and chopped nuts. We take this theme and combine pâte à bombe, meringue and whipped cream with nougatine and candied fruits to create a creamy melt-in-the-mouth iced parfait. This is a good parfait to make around Christmas when you can buy excellent candied fruits from food halls, delis and supermarkets. The effect is eye catching, especially if you serve the parfait with a fresh minty mango salsa – one of my favourites.

1 First, make the nougatine. Put the sugar and water in a heavy-based saucepan and dissolve over a low heat, stirring occasionally with a wooden spoon until the sugar solution is clear. Increase the heat and cook the syrup to a light caramel colour, about 7 minutes. Remove from the heat and mix in the hazelnuts. Immediately tip on to a non-stick baking tray, spread level and leave to cool.

2 Make the pâte à bombe for the parfait and set aside.

3 When the nougatine is cold and brittle, break it into pieces and crush with a rolling pin. Wash the candied fruits in warm water to remove excess sugar. Drain and pat dry, then chop into 1cm pieces.

4 Put the cream in a bowl and three-quarters whip until softly stiff. In another bowl, whisk the egg whites with the lemon juice until stiff then gradually whisk in the caster sugar to make a firm, glossy meringue.

5 Fold the pâte à bombe and whipped cream together, then fold in the meringue. Add the nougatine, candied fruits, sultanas and pistachios, and fold together until just evenly mixed. Spoon into a 1.2 litre loaf tin or individual moulds and freeze until firm.

6 To unmould the parfait, dip individual moulds into warm water for a second, then turn out on to serving plates. Invert a large parfait on to a board and allow to soften for 5–10 minutes before slicing.

SERVES 6–8

NOUGATINE:

150g caster sugar

3 tablespoons water

3 tablespoons hazelnuts

PARFAIT:

1 quantity Pâte à bombe (page 198)

300ml double cream

2 large free-range egg whites

squeeze of lemon juice

80g caster sugar

FRUIT AND NUTS:

100g candied fruits, such as orange slices, angelica and pineapple

3 tablespoons sultanas

40g unsalted pistachios, roughly chopped

LUSCIOUS DRIZZLED WITH MANGO AND MINT SALSA (PAGE 12)

Chestnut parfait

SERVES 6–8

1 quantity Pâte à bombe (page 198)

200g can sweetened chestnut purée

50g soft brown sugar

2 tablespoons crème de châtaigne (chestnut liqueur), or rum

300ml double cream, lightly whipped

4 marrons glacés, chopped (optional)

NICE WITH ROASTED BLACK FIGS WITH SPICED BALSAMIC SYRUP (PAGE 42), OR WITH CHRISTMAS PUDDING OR MINCE PIES

If you like nut ice creams, do try this one. It is a simplified version of my fresh chestnut parfait – flavoured with sweetened chestnut purée and marrons glacés, rather than fresh nuts. You should find marrons glacés in a good food hall or deli, at a price, though you can sometimes buy them singly. If possible, track down a bottle of chestnut liqueur too.

1 Make the pâte à bombe and chill.

2 Whizz the chestnut purée in a food processor or blender with the sugar and liqueur or rum until very smooth and creamy. Lightly whip the cream in a bowl until softly peaking.

3 Lightly fold the chestnut mixture into the pâte à bombe, followed by the whipped cream and chopped marrons glacés, if using. Spoon into a 1 litre mould and freeze until firm.

4 To unmould the parfait, dip the mould into warm water for a few seconds, then invert on to a board. Allow the parfait to soften for 5–10 minutes. Serve cut into slices.

Jasmine tea and lime parfait

SERVES 6–8

300ml double cream

5g jasmine tea leaves

125g caster sugar

1 quantity Pâte à bombe (page 198)

juice of 4 limes

4 tablespoons pineapple juice

2 large free-range egg whites

1 teaspoon lemon juice

As this has a light, summery flavour, you'll find it delectable with fruits such as peaches, nectarines and red berries.

1 Put half of the cream in a small pan with the tea leaves and 25g of the sugar. Bring just to the boil, stirring. Pour into a jug and allow to cool, then chill for about 24 hours. Strain through a fine sieve into a bowl.

2 Make the pâte à bombe and set aside. Put the lime and pineapple juices in a small pan and boil until reduced by half. Cool, then mix into the pâte à bombe with the infused cream.

3 In another bowl, whisk the egg whites with the lemon juice until softly stiff, then gradually whisk in the remaining sugar until you have a firm, glossy meringue. Fold this into the lime and pâte à bombe mixture.

4 Whip the remaining cream until it just begins to thicken, then carefully fold this in too, keeping the mixture nice and light. Pour into a 1 litre mould and freeze until firm.

5 To unmould, dip into warm water for a few seconds, then invert on to a board. Allow the parfait to soften for 5–10 minutes. Serve cut into slices.

Mango and passion fruit parfait

Sweet, fragrant mangoes taste superb. Fortunately they are nearly always in the shops when we need them, winging their way from exotic far-flung corners. In midsummer Indian mangoes are at their most perfumed – the Alphonso variety is deemed to be the finest – your local Asian food store should be a good source of supply. To heighten the fragrance, I add fresh passion fruit juice.

1 Make the pâte à bombe and set aside.

2 Peel the mangoes then cut the flesh from the stone; you should have about 350g. Chop roughly and place in a food processor.

3 Halve the passion fruit and scoop out the pulp into the processor. Whizz until smooth, scraping down the sides once or twice. Rub the fruit pulp through a fine sieve into a bowl, cover and chill.

4 Whisk the egg whites and lemon juice in a bowl until softly stiff, then gradually whisk in the sugar until you have a smooth, glossy meringue. Whip the cream in another bowl until softly stiff.

5 Fold the chilled fruit pulp into the pâte à bombe, then fold this mixture into the meringue. Finally fold in the whipped cream.

6 Spoon into a 1.2 litre mould or 8–10 individual moulds, such as darioles or ramekins. Freeze until firm.

7 To serve, unmould a large parfait by dipping the mould into warm water for a few seconds, then turn out on to a board. Allow to soften for 5–10 minutes before slicing. Unmould individual parfaits straight on to serving plates.

SERVES 8

1 quantity Pâte à bombe (page 198)

2 large ripe mangoes

3 ripe, wrinkled passion fruit

2 large free-range egg whites

tiny squeeze of lemon juice

100g caster sugar

250ml double cream

SURROUND WITH TRICKLES OF RASPBERRY, STRAWBERRY OR KIWI COULIS (PAGE 11). DELIGHTFUL WITH NUT TUILES (PAGE 170) OR LANGUES DE CHAT (PAGE 173)

White peach parfaits

Make this lovely refreshing parfait at the height of summer when white peaches – my all-time favourites – are in season. Out of season, you can use other full flavoured juicy peaches or nectarines.

1 Make the pâte à bombe and set aside. Prepare the stock syrup and add the basil leaves while it is hot; leave to steep as the syrup cools for about 30 minutes, then strain.

2 Meanwhile, skin the peaches: immerse them in boiling water for 30 seconds, then into ice-cold water. Lift out and peel, then halve and stone them.

3 Gently poach the peach halves in the syrup for 10 minutes, then drain (the syrup can be used again). Purée the peaches in a blender or food processor, turn into a bowl and mix in the crème de pêche.

4 In another bowl, whisk the egg whites with the lemon juice until softly stiff, then gradually whisk in the sugar to make a firm, glossy meringue.

5 Whip the cream until it just holds its shape, then fold into the peach purée together with the meringue.

6 Spoon into a 1.2 litre mould or 8–10 individual moulds, such as darioles or ramekins. Freeze until solid.

7 To serve, unmould a large parfait by dipping the mould into warm water for a few seconds, then turn out on to a board and allow to soften for 5–10 minutes before slicing. Unmould individual parfaits straight on to serving plates. Surround with oven-dried peach slices and top with sugar-crusted basil leaves if you like.

SUGAR-CRUSTED LEAVES Dip small basil, mint or coriander leaves in lightly beaten egg white, then dust liberally with caster sugar. Place on a tray lined with baking parchment and leave to dry overnight in a warm dry spot, such as an airing cupboard.

SERVES 8–10
1 quantity Pâte à bombe (page 198)
500ml Stock syrup (page 200)
6 large basil leaves
4 large white peaches
1 tablespoon crème de pêche
2 medium free-range egg whites
squeeze of lemon juice
100g caster sugar
150ml double cream
TO SERVE (OPTIONAL):
Sugar-crusted basil leaves (see below left)
Oven-dried peach slices (page 46)

SENSATIONAL PARTNERED BY SLOW-ROASTED PEACHES WITH ORANGE CARAMEL SAUCE (PAGE 34)

SORBETS

Sorbets are wonderfully refreshing, fine-textured water ices. They are best made in an ice cream machine so they churn to a silky smoothness that a spoon can glide through. They have the base of a stock syrup – plain or flavoured, depending on the recipe. For optimum flavour, serve sorbets shortly after freezing, or at least within a week. If frozen in advance you will need to soften the sorbet at room temperature for about 10 minutes before serving. Otherwise you will find it too hard to scoop or shave with a spoon.

Strawberry sorbet

MAKES ABOUT 750ml
500g strawberries, hulled
juice of 1 large lemon
200ml water
250g caster sugar
3 tablespoons liquid glucose

Choose ripe, fragrant homegrown berries at the height of their season for this mouth-watering sorbet. They really do make a difference to the flavour and it's amazing how the lemon juice intensifies it still further. Serve in elegant glasses, accompanied by dessert biscuits if you like.

1 Put the strawberries and lemon juice into a food processor or blender and whizz to a purée. Tip into a saucepan, bring to the boil and boil until reduced by half. Cool slightly, then rub the pulp through a sieve into a bowl to remove the seeds. Set aside to cool completely.
2 Meanwhile, put the water, sugar and glucose in a heavy-based saucepan and heat gently until the sugar has dissolved and the syrup is clear. Bring to the boil and boil for 5 minutes. Cool.
3 Add the syrup to the strawberry purée and stir to combine. Cover and chill thoroughly.
4 Churn the mixture in an ice cream machine until almost frozen, then scoop into a suitable container and freeze until firm. Alternatively, freeze in a shallow container, beating 2 or 3 times during freezing. Serve in scoops or shavings.

Three melon sorbet

A melt-in-the-mouth melange of melons is the perfect way to round off a meal lightly. Late summer is the ideal time to make this sorbet, when there is an abundance of ripe fragrant melons. You do need three different varieties for the best balance of flavours. To make sure they are ripe and full of juicy flavour, give them a good sniff – they should exude a lovely scent. Orange-fleshed Charentais melon and Grenadine give the sorbet a pretty pink colour.

MAKES ABOUT 2 LITRES
1 ripe Charentais or Cantaloupe melon
1 ripe honeydew melon
1 ripe Galia melon
500ml water
350g caster sugar
3 tablespoons liquid glucose
juice of 1 lemon
1¹/₂ tablespoons Grenadine

1 Halve all 3 melons and discard the seeds. Scoop the flesh together with any overflowing juices, into a food processor and whizz to a purée; transfer to a bowl. (You may need to do this in batches.) Cover and chill.
2 Put the water, sugar and glucose in a heavy-based saucepan and heat gently until the sugar has dissolved. Bring to the boil and boil for 2–3 minutes. Cool, then mix in the lemon juice and Grenadine. Chill.
3 Add the syrup to the melon purée and stir together. Churn in an ice cream machine until almost firm, then freeze in a suitable container. Or freeze in a shallow container, beating 2 or 3 times during freezing. Serve the sorbet in scoops or shavings.

Raspberry sorbet

This is a beautiful purple-red sorbet that I could just eat and eat. You do need to use fresh homegrown raspberries in season and naturally I prefer Scottish ones – they're the best. The syrup is strong to accentuate the flavour of the fruit.

MAKES ABOUT 1 LITRE
700g raspberries
juice of 1 small lemon
300ml water
200g caster sugar
3 tablespoons liquid glucose

1 Put the raspberries in a food processor with the lemon juice. Whizz to a smooth purée then transfer to a bowl, cover and chill.
2 Meanwhile, put the water and sugar in a heavy-based pan and dissolve over a low heat. When the syrup is clear, increase the heat to medium and boil for 5 minutes. Stir in the glucose and cool.
3 Mix the cooled sugar syrup with the raspberry purée. Pass through a sieve into a bowl to remove the seeds, rubbing the mixture through with the back of the ladle.
4 Churn in an ice cream machine until almost frozen solid, then transfer to a rigid plastic container and put in the freezer. Alternatively, freeze in a shallow container, beating 2 or 3 times during freezing. Serve in scoops or shavings.

Fromage frais sorbet

MAKES 1 LITRE

350ml water

225g caster sugar

3 tablespoons liquid glucose

2 tablespoons lemon juice

250g fromage frais

3 tablespoons crème fraîche

3 tablespoons natural yogurt

3 tablespoons double cream

SERVE WITH A SALAD OF SLICED
STRAWBERRIES OR KIWI FRUIT FOR A
MOUTH-WATERING LIGHT DESSERT

This is truly refreshing – wonderful served between courses and certainly more inviting than the over-sweet lemon sorbet served in some restaurants. I specify fromage frais, but you could substitute mascarpone for a richer, creamier sorbet.

1 Put the water, sugar and glucose in a heavy-based saucepan over a low heat. Once the sugar has dissolved, increase the heat and boil for 3 minutes. Cool and then stir in the lemon juice. Chill.

2 Beat the fromage frais, crème fraîche, yogurt and cream together in a bowl until smooth and creamy. Cover and chill.

3 When ready to freeze, add the syrup to the fromage frais mixture and stir to combine.

4 Churn in an ice cream machine until almost firm, then transfer to a suitable container, seal and freeze. If you do not have an ice cream maker, freeze in a shallow container, beating 2 or 3 times during freezing. Serve the sorbet in scoops or shavings.

Banana and passion fruit sorbet

MAKES ABOUT 1 LITRE

8 ripe passion fruit

4 large, ripe bananas

1 teaspoon grated lemon zest

300ml water

125g caster sugar

3 tablespoons liquid glucose

This is one of the most popular sorbets in my restaurant. Flavourful fruit is the key to success. Select passion fruit with wrinkled skins – an indication that they are mature. Choose well ripened bananas too – those with spotty skins should be full of flavour.

1 Halve the passion fruit, scoop out the pulp into a small pan and warm gently (this helps to loosen the juicy flesh from the seeds). Rub through a small sieve into a bowl, using a wooden spoon; discard the seeds.

2 Mash the bananas with a fork to a purée, then add to the passion fruit juice with the lemon zest and mix well.

3 Transfer to a saucepan and add the water, sugar and glucose. Bring to the boil, stirring, then simmer for a minute or two. Allow to cool, then cover and chill.

4 Churn in an ice cream machine until creamy and almost firm, then transfer to a freezer container, seal and put into the freezer. If you do not have an ice cream machine, freeze the mixture in a shallow container, beating 2 or 3 times during freezing.

5 Serve the sorbet slightly softened. If frozen well ahead, allow to stand at room temperature for 10 minutes before scooping.

Green apple sorbet

The pale green colour of this sorbet is so tempting, it's almost virginal, and the clean, fruity taste is divine. Serve on its own, or with apple tart tatin, roasted fruits or a bowl of fresh strawberries.

1 Quarter and core the apples, but do not peel, then toss with the lemon juice. Place in a single layer in a shallow plastic container and freeze for a good hour (this helps to intensify the colour).
2 Meanwhile, dissolve the sugar in the water in a heavy-based saucepan over a low heat. Bring to the boil and cook on a medium heat for 5 minutes. Cool, then mix in the glucose.
3 Whizz the ice-cold apples in a food processor, gradually adding about a third of the syrup to make a fine purée. Scrape down the sides of the bowl once or twice as you do this.
4 Mix in the rest of the syrup then pass through a sieve into a bowl, rubbing with the back of a ladle to extract as much juice as possible.
5 Transfer to an ice cream machine. Churn until almost solid, then transfer to a rigid plastic container, seal and freeze. Alternatively, freeze the mixture in a shallow container, beating 2 or 3 times during freezing. Serve in scoops or shaped into quenelles.

MAKES ABOUT 1.2 LITRES
4 large Granny Smith apples
juice of 1 large lemon
200g caster sugar
400ml water
4 tablespoons liquid glucose

Tomato and basil sorbet

Botanically, tomatoes are fruits, so why not serve them as a dessert? This sorbet is excellent for cleansing palates between courses, too. And, what a colour! The more flavourful the tomatoes, the better the sorbet.

1 Whizz the tomatoes in a food processor or blender with the salt, then rub through a sieve into a bowl. Cover and chill overnight.
2 Put the water, sugar and glucose in a heavy-based saucepan and heat gently until the sugar has dissolved and the syrup is clear. Bring to the boil and boil for a couple of minutes. Take off the heat, add the basil leaves and leave to steep in the hot syrup as it cools. Strain and chill.
3 When ready to freeze, combine the puréed tomatoes and infused syrup. Churn in an ice cream machine until almost firm, then transfer to a suitable container, seal and pop into the freezer. Or freeze in a shallow container, beating 2 or 3 times during freezing.
4 Serve in small scoops, or scrape shavings into elegant cocktail glasses. Top with perky basil sprigs to serve.

MAKES 1 LITRE
10 large ripe plum tomatoes
$\frac{1}{4}$ teaspoon fine sea salt
200ml water
250g caster sugar
3 tablespoons liquid glucose
about 30g fresh basil leaves, plus tiny sprigs
  to serve

EXCELLENT SERVED AS A PALATE CLEANSER
BETWEEN COURSES

Pink grapefruit sorbet

MAKES ABOUT 1.5 LITRES

5 ripe pink grapefruit

2 white grapefruit

2 large oranges

270g caster sugar

450ml water

juice of 1 lemon

3 tablespoons Campari

I'm keen to make the most of pink grapefruit when they come into season, and use them in both sweet and savoury dishes. It's the appeal of those pink teardrop segments with their tangy sweet-sour flavour. I combine them with complementary citrus fruits and a good shot of Campari to make this stimulating sorbet.

1 Using a sharp knife, cut the peel and white pith from all the grapefruit and oranges, then cut between the membranes to release the segments. Place these in a food processor and whizz to a juicy purée, then rub through a sieve into a bowl. (You may need to do this in batches.) Cover and chill.

2 Dissolve the sugar in the water in a heavy-based saucepan over a low heat, then increase the heat and boil for a couple of minutes. Cool. Stir the lemon juice and Campari into the cooled sugar syrup, then chill.

3 Mix the citrus juice and syrup together. Churn in an ice cream machine until almost firm, then freeze in a suitable container. Alternatively, freeze in a shallow container beating 2 or 3 times during freezing. Serve in scoops or shavings.

Black and blue fruit sorbet

MAKES ABOUT 1 LITRE

500g fresh blackcurrants, stalks removed

125g wild blackberries, hulled

125g blueberries

200ml water

250g caster sugar

3 tablespoons liquid glucose

juice of 2 lemons

As the appearance of wild blackberries coincides with the end of the blackcurrant season, I crush them together with blueberries and a lemony syrup to make this delightful water ice. You can pick 'brambles' or wild blackberries in woodlands and hedgerows from the end of July.

1 Wash the blackcurrants and berries well, keeping them separate, then drain. Put the blackcurrants into a saucepan and heat gently until the skins burst open. Continue to simmer for a further 2–3 minutes. Remove from the heat and set aside to cool.

2 Put the water, sugar and glucose in a heavy-based pan and heat gently until the sugar has dissolved and the syrup is clear. Bring to the boil and boil for 2–3 minutes. Cool, then mix in the lemon juice. Chill.

3 Tip the blackcurrants into a food processor or blender, add the black and blueberries and purée to a pulp. Transfer to a bowl and chill.

4 Combine the chilled purée and syrup. Churn in an ice cream machine until almost firm, then freeze in a suitable container. Or freeze in a shallow container, beating during freezing. Serve in scoops or shavings.

Mandarin sorbet

Mandarins have a full, sweet flavour and make a vibrant orange sorbet. This is outstanding with strawberries, but also good as a dessert in its own right – served with little crisp shortbreads. You can use clementines before mandarins come into season.

MAKES ABOUT 1 LITRE
1.5kg mandarins
juice of 2 lemons
200g caster sugar
400ml water
3 tablespoons liquid glucose

1 Peel the mandarins and remove as much of the pith as possible. Whizz the mandarins with the lemon juice in a food processor to a smooth purée, scraping down the sides a couple of times. (You may need to do this in batches.)

2 Meanwhile, dissolve the sugar in the water in a heavy-based saucepan over a low heat. Once clear, increase the heat to medium and boil for 5 minutes. Set aside to cool.

3 Tip the mandarin purée into a large jug and mix in the cooled syrup and glucose. Pass the mixture through a sieve into a bowl, rubbing it through with the back of a ladle. Cover and chill.

4 Churn in an ice cream machine until almost solid; transfer to a suitable container to store in the freezer. Or freeze in a shallow container, beating 2 or 3 times during freezing. Serve in scoops.

Dark chocolate and brandy sorbet

With the texture of a clean sorbet and the flavour of dark, bitter chocolate, this is an unusual sorbet to say the least. It is certainly lighter than an ice cream and has far fewer calories. This is one sorbet that can only be made in an electric machine, because constant stirring is essential for a creamy chocolate texture. I like to serve it with Roasted pineapple (page 38) or Caramelised mango slices (page 42).

MAKES ABOUT 800ml
250ml milk
250ml water
150g caster sugar
3 tablespoons liquid glucose
3 tablespoons brandy
200g dark chocolate (about 60% cocoa solids)

1 Put the milk, water, sugar and glucose into a heavy-based saucepan and bring slowly to the boil, stirring until dissolved. Remove from the heat and mix in the brandy.

2 Break the chocolate into pieces and add to the milk mixture, stirring until melted. Return to the heat and bring back to a gentle boil. Cook for a minute or two, making sure it doesn't boil over, then remove from the heat.

3 Cool, stirring once or twice to stop a skin forming.

4 Churn the mixture in an ice cream machine until it is firm and creamy. Serve in scoops or shaped into quenelles.

GRANITAS

As the name suggests, these are grainy-textured water ices – wonderfully refreshing for those scorching hot summer days when you want their cooling effect to linger longer. Because they are only lightly beaten with a fork as they freeze, granitas are almost effortless to make – and even more so to eat. Unlike fine-textured ice creams and sorbets, they have large ice crystals. Perhaps best described as an iced slush, granitas should be eaten almost as soon as they are frozen. The texture should be decidedly crunchy.

A light pineapple granita

A fully ripened pineapple is full of juicy sweetness and perfect for turning into a light water ice. Even a slightly overripe pineapple can be put to good use here. The ingredients are so simple – puréed pineapple flesh, water and sugar.

SERVES 4–6
1 large ripe sweet pineapple
250ml water
75g caster sugar

1 Cut the top and bottom off the pineapple, then stand it upright on a board and cut away the peel.
2 Next, cut out the 'eyes'. The easiest way to do this is to cut out narrow wedges in a spiral fashion, following the contours of the 'eyes' (as illustrated). Quarter the pineapple lengthways and cut out the hard central core. Roughly chop the pineapple flesh and put into a food processor or blender with the water and sugar. Whizz to a pulp.
3 Rinse a large square of muslin in cold water and use to line a large sieve, placed over a bowl. Tip the fruit pulp into the sieve and allow the juice to drip through; this may take 2–3 hours but achieves a crystal clear liquid. You can speed up the process if necessary, by gathering the ends of the muslin and twisting gently to squeeze out the juice.
4 When you have extracted as much juice as possible, pour it into a shallow freezer container and place in the freezer for about 2 hours until it is frozen on the base and sides. Take out of the freezer and beat lightly with a fork to mix the frozen crystals with the liquid. Return to the freezer, beating lightly twice more during freezing to achieve a granular texture.
5 When ready to serve, scrape shavings off the frozen granita block with a strong spoon. Serve immediately, in wine glasses.

Lemon grass granita

SERVES 6–8

500ml water
125g caster sugar
3 tablespoons liquid glucose
juice of 1 lemon
4 lemon grass stalks, chopped
1 large fresh lemon balm or spearmint sprig
grated zest of 1 lime or 1 small lemon

A truly refreshing water ice with a subtle fragrance and hint of tropical flavour. Serve in elegant wine glasses or sundae dishes.

1 Heat the water, sugar and glucose slowly in a heavy-based saucepan, stirring occasionally, until the sugar has dissolved. Increase the heat and boil the syrup for about 3 minutes.

2 Take off the heat and stir in the lemon juice, lemon grass, herbs and citrus zest. Set aside to infuse until cold.

3 Strain the infused syrup into a shallow freezer container. Freeze until almost solid, beating it lightly with a fork 2 or 3 times as it freezes.

4 To serve, scrape shavings off the frozen block of granita, using a strong spoon. Serve immediately.

Espresso coffee granita

SERVES 6–8

100g sugar
150ml water
2 cardamom pods
1 or 2 strips of orange zest
500ml strong fresh coffee, cooled

This is the ultimate iced coffee. First you need to make some very strong coffee, then blend it with stock syrup in the proportion of 2 to 1. If you have a home espresso machine, this recipe is particularly appropriate. The finer the flavour of the coffee the better the granita. I infuse it with cardamom and orange zest to give it an Arabic slant, but you can omit these if you prefer.

1 Put the sugar and water in a saucepan over a low heat, stirring occasionally, until dissolved. Add the cardamom pods and orange zest and boil for 3 minutes. Remove from the heat, cool for 1 hour and then discard the cardamom pods and orange zest.

2 Mix the coffee with the infused syrup and chill.

3 Transfer to a shallow rigid container and freeze for 2–3 hours until partially frozen. Take the semi-frozen granita from the freezer and stir the frozen crystals into the liquid, using a fork; return to the freezer. Beat lightly twice more during freezing to achieve a granular texture.

4 To serve, scrape shavings off the frozen block of granita with a strong spoon. Serve at once.

mousses, bavarois and soufflés

MOUSSES

All of my mousses are created from a pâte à bombe base, which is basically egg yolks whisked with a sugar syrup until thick and creamy. This is flavoured according to the recipe and combined with a firm meringue and whipped cream. There is no setting agent involved, so the texture is smooth and silky. One of the secrets of success is to make sure the components are similar in texture. Your cream for example, should be three-quarters whipped; your meringue needs to be softly stiff. Obligingly pâte à bombe is always softly stiff. Equally important, the elements should be at the same (room) temperature when you combine them.

These mousses are not suitable for setting in moulds and turning out. They are best served in small glasses, or spooned from a large serving bowl, or shaped into soft quenelles (see page 50).

Note: Mousses – like bavarois and meringues – contain lightly cooked egg. Although the risk of salmonella is small, those who are particularly vulnerable should avoid these desserts.

Pâte à bombe base

MAKES ABOUT 350ml
100ml water
150g caster sugar
5 large free-range egg yolks

This is the base recipe for all the mousses in this chapter. A sugar thermometer is helpful for determining when the syrup reaches the correct temperature. Prepare the pâte à bombe according to the basic method (see page 198), making sure you whisk it until it is really thick and glossy. The pâte à bombe must be at room temperature when you incorporate it into the mousse mixture.

Italian meringue base

MAKES ABOUT 600ml
120g caster sugar
1 teaspoon liquid glucose
2 tablespoons water
2 large free-range egg whites

Made by whisking a hot sugar syrup into whisked egg whites, this mixture is more stable than the more familiar French meringue. As it holds up well ahead of time, it's ideal for mousses. Italian meringue is often combined with pâte à bombe, which conveniently uses up some of the egg whites. Prepare the meringue according to the basic method (see page 197). Once the syrup is all incorporated, continue to whisk until the meringue cools to room temperature.

Pineapple and star anise mousse

A pineapple mousse cannot be set with gelatine because the fruit contains an enzyme that breaks down the protein responsible for setting. My soft set, gelatine-free mousse is the ideal solution – and it tastes divine.

1 Peel the pineapple and cut out the 'eyes'. Quarter lengthways, then cut out and discard the hard central core. Roughly chop the pineapple flesh and pat dry on kitchen paper. Weigh 250g pineapple cubes for the mousse. (Refrigerate any remaining pineapple to use in a fruit salad.)
2 Heat a large heavy-based frying pan until you can feel a strong heat rising. Toss the pineapple in the sugar to coat each piece, then scatter over the base of the hot pan; add the star anise too. The fruit should start to brown quickly. Do not stir until the pieces start to caramelise. Once all the pineapple is nicely golden brown and syrupy, add the rum and cook until reduced right down. Remove from the heat and cool.
3 Make the pâte à bombe and meringue and cool both mixtures.
4 When the fruit is cool, discard the star anise and purée the flesh in a food processor or blender.
5 Fold the pineapple purée into the meringue using a spatula or large metal spoon, then fold in the pâte à bombe.
6 Lastly, whip the cream in a bowl until softly stiff and fold into the mousse mixture, using a metal spoon. Spoon into individual dishes or one large glass serving bowl. Chill until lightly firm.

SERVES 4–6

1 medium, ripe sweet pineapple, or 250g fresh pineapple cubes
50g caster sugar
2 star anise
2 tablespoons white rum
1 quantity Pâte à bombe base (page 86)
1 quantity Italian meringue base (page 86)
200ml double cream

Mango and dark chocolate mousse

SERVES 6

1 quantity Pâte à bombe base (page 86)

1 quantity Italian meringue base (page 86)

2 fresh apricots, or 4 mi-cuit (no-need-to-soak)
   dried apricots

1 large mango, ripe but not soft

1 tablespoon chopped fresh mint

200g dark chocolate (at least 60% cocoa solids)

300ml double cream

TOP WITH CARAMELISED MANGO SLICES
(PAGE 42) TO SERVE, AS ILLUSTRATED

The unlikely combination of flavours in this recipe comes together beautifully. Why not serve it as a special party mousse?

1 Make up the pâte à bombe and meringue mixtures and cool both.
2 If using fresh apricots, halve and stone, then cut into quarters. Peel and roughly chop the mango, discarding the stone. Blend the chopped mango and fresh (or mi-cuit) apricots to a purée in a blender or food processor. Pass through a sieve into a bowl, rubbing the purée through with the back of a ladle. Stir in the mint.
3 Melt the chocolate in a heatproof bowl over a pan of simmering water, or in the microwave (see page 183), and stir until smooth. Cool to room temperature, stirring occasionally.
4 Fold the fruit purée into the pâte à bombe. Lightly fold the cooled chocolate into the meringue, then fold in the creamy fruit mixture.
5 Finally, whip the cream until softly stiff and fold into the mousse. Spoon into individual glasses or one large bowl and chill to set.

Mandarin orange, thyme and mint mousse

SERVES 6

about 12 mandarin oranges

grated zest of 1 lemon

2 fresh thyme sprigs (preferably to include a
   sprig of lemon thyme)

4 large fresh mint leaves, finely chopped

1 quantity Pâte à bombe base (page 86)

1 quantity Italian meringue base (page 86)

300ml double cream

Make this refreshing soft-set mousse after Christmas when mandarins are in season, or you could use clementines in the festive season. At other times, simply use 500ml freshly squeezed orange juice and standard orange zest.

1 Grate the zest from 4 of the mandarins and reserve. Halve all the fruit and squeeze the juice. (Here an electric juicer is helpful if you have one.) You should have 500ml juice.
2 Pour the mandarin juice into a saucepan and boil to reduce to 200ml. Stir in the citrus zests, thyme and mint and leave to infuse until cool.
3 Make the pâte à bombe and meringue and cool both.
4 Strain the infused fruit juice through a fine sieve into a bowl, rubbing with the back of a ladle.
5 Stir the mandarin juice into the pâte à bombe until smooth, then fold in the meringue. Finally, whip the cream in a bowl until softly stiff and fold into the mousse. Divide between individual dishes or spoon into one large bowl. Chill until softly set.

Apricot and cinnamon mousse

I like to take advantage of fresh apricots when they appear, especially the wonderful pink-blushed fruits that arrive from France in midsummer. This mousse has an inviting spicy flavour, intensified by caramelising the fruit.

1 Halve and stone the apricots, then cut into quarters. Heat a large heavy-based frying pan until you can feel a strong heat rising. Toss the fruits in the sugar until they are evenly coated.
2 Add the apricots to the pan in a single layer and cook until nicely caramelised on both sides; don't stir too often. Tip into a bowl, mix in the spices and cool to room temperature, stirring once or twice.
3 Meanwhile, make the pâte à bombe and meringue and cool.
4 Discard the cinnamon sticks (if used) and blend the apricots to a purée in a food processor or blender.
5 Whip the cream in a bowl until it stands in peaks (slightly firmer than is usual for a mousse) and fold in the apricot purée.
6 Fold the pâte à bombe and meringue together, then fold in the creamy apricot mixture. Spoon into individual dishes or one large bowl and chill before serving.

Variation
When apricots are out of season, poach 300g mi-cuit (no-need-to-soak) dried apricots in 150ml water with the sugar and spices for 2–3 minutes or until soft; remove whole spices. Blend to a purée. Continue as above.

SERVES 6–8
500g ripe (but not soft) apricots
50g caster sugar
3 cinnamon sticks, or $^3/_4$ teaspoon ground cinnamon
$^1/_2$ teaspoon freshly grated nutmeg
1 quantity Pâte à bombe base (page 86)
1 quantity Italian meringue base (page 86)
300ml double cream

DELICIOUS TOPPED WITH GLAZED APRICOTS (PAGE 43) AND ROUGHLY CRUSHED HONEYCOMB (PAGE 201) AS ILLUSTRATED

Milk chocolate and nutmeg mousse

Quality milk chocolate, such as Jivara, is a revelation and makes a fine mousse. A good sprinkling of fresh nutmeg enhances the flavour.

1 Melt the chocolate in a heatproof bowl over a pan of simmering water, or in the microwave (see page 183), and stir until smooth. Cool to room temperature, stirring occasionally.
2 Make up the pâte à bombe and meringue mixtures and leave to cool.
3 Gently fold the melted chocolate and nutmeg into the pâte à bombe, then fold in the meringue.
4 Finally, whip the cream until softly stiff and fold into the mixture. Spoon into individual dishes or a serving bowl. Chill to set.

SERVES 6–8
300g good quality milk chocolate
1 quantity Pâte à bombe base (page 86)
1 quantity Italian meringue base (page 86)
1 teaspoon freshly grated nutmeg
300ml double cream

BAVAROIS

Bavarois are melt-in-the-mouth rich mixtures – mostly fruit flavoured – set in little moulds to be turned out, or in a large bowl to be scooped into quenelles for serving. There are many great classic bavarois, but I enjoy experimenting with original flavour combinations, and variations on established favourites.

The base for a bavarois is crème anglaise into which dissolved gelatine is stirred. This is combined with a fruit purée or other flavouring mixture, then enriched with softly whipped cream and French meringue. I always use leaf gelatine. It is easy to use – you simply soften the sheets in cold water before slipping them into the hot custard, whisking lightly until they melt. If necessary, you can substitute powdered gelatine: one 11g sachet is equivalent to 4 sheets of leaf gelatine.

Bavarois base

MAKES ABOUT 600ml
200ml milk
200ml double cream
100g caster sugar
6 large free-range egg yolks
4 sheets of leaf gelatine

This crème anglaise – with added gelatine – forms the base for all of the subsequent bavarois recipes.

1 Put the milk and cream in a heavy-based pan with 1 tablespoon of the sugar and heat until scalding.
2 Meanwhile, whisk the egg yolks and remaining sugar together in a large bowl to a pale, thick cream. When the creamy milk is just starting to rise up the side of the pan, pour a third of it in small amounts on to the egg and sugar mix, whisking as you do so. Return this mixture to the pan.
3 Immerse the leaf gelatine in a bowl of cold water (halving it first if necessary) and leave to soften for about 5 minutes.
4 Meanwhile, cook the crème anglaise on the lowest possible heat, stirring with a wooden spoon for about 5 minutes, until the custard is slightly thickened. If you draw a line down the back of the spoon with your finger, it should leave an impression.
5 Lift the gelatine sheets from the bowl, squeeze gently to remove excess water then slip into the warm crème anglaise and whisk until they have dissolved. Pass through a sieve into a bowl and set aside to cool, stirring once or twice. Use as required.

Apricot and passion fruit bavarois

Fresh, concentrated passion fruit juice gives this bavarois a wonderful depth of flavour, justifying the time it takes to prepare it. However, you could substitute 1 tablespoon orange flower water for a quicker alternative; simply add at stage 4 with the apricots.

1 Make up the bavarois base and set aside to cool.

2 Snip the apricots into pieces. Place in a bowl, cover with boiling water and leave for 10 minutes, then drain well.

3 Halve the passion fruit and scoop out the pulp into a saucepan. Stir in the orange juice, bring to the boil and boil until reduced to 150ml. Pass through a sieve into a bowl, rubbing with a wooden spoon to extract as much juice as possible.

4 Return the passion fruit juice to the saucepan and add the apricots. Bring to the boil and simmer gently for 5 minutes. Cool slightly, then purée in a blender or food processor. Set aside to cool.

5 Briskly stir the fruit purée into the cooled bavarois base. Chill lightly until it is just on the point of setting around the sides.

6 Whip the cream until softly stiff, then fold into the bavarois mixture with a large metal spoon. Pour into lightly oiled individual moulds or a large bowl. Chill until set.

To turn out a bavarois: To ensure your bavarois will turn out easily, wipe the inside of the mould lightly with almond oil before filling. Make sure the bavarois is firmly set before turning it out. Dip the mould into a bowl of just-boiled water, hold to the count of three, then remove. Gently ease the set mixture away from the sides of the mould with your fingertips. Invert on to a small wet plate, shake firmly and the bavarois should just plop out. If it doesn't, then repeat the process until it does.

SERVES 8–10

1 quantity Bavarois base (page 92)

250g mi-cuit (no-need-to-soak) dried apricots

4 ripe, wrinkled passion fruit

200ml fresh orange juice

200ml double cream

Green apple and grapefruit bavarois

SERVES 8–10

100ml grapefruit juice (not pink)

juice of 1 lemon

4 Granny Smith apples

1 quantity Bavarois base (page 92)

200ml double cream

FOR AN IMPRESSIVE FINALE, TOP WITH
DRIED APPLE SLICES (PAGE 46) AND A
SCOOP OF GREEN APPLE SORBET (PAGE 77)

These individual bavarois – speckled green with flecks of apple skin – look really pretty. To enhance the appearance, I suggest you freeze the freshly prepared apple, with skin, a day ahead. This sets the colour.

1 Put the grapefruit and lemon juices into a bowl. Quarter and core one apple at a time, halve each quarter and immediately toss in the citrus juices to prevent discoloration. Using a slotted spoon, transfer the apple pieces to a colander set over a bowl to drain. Repeat with the remaining apples; reserve and chill the juice.

2 Once all of the apples are prepared, lay the pieces out in a single layer on a small baking sheet or large plate and freeze overnight.

3 The next day, partially thaw the apples. Meanwhile, make the bavarois base and cool.

4 Whizz the apple pieces in a food processor or blender with the reserved juice until you have a very smooth mix. (I suggest you do this in batches to avoid putting a strain on your machine.) Pour the frozen slurry (for that is what it is) into a bowl and keep chilled.

5 Whip the cream in a bowl until softly stiff. Now, beat the cold apple purée into the cooled bavarois base and then immediately fold in the whipped cream. Spoon into lightly oiled individual moulds or a large bowl and chill in the fridge to set.

Caramelised banana bavarois

This takes baked bananas to new heights. It is seriously good but, be warned, you may find you can't resist eating it. Your bananas should be well ripened with spotty skins, but not soft.

1 Heat a large heavy-based frying pan until you can feel a strong heat rising. Meanwhile, peel the bananas and quarter lengthways. Toss half of them in the caster sugar and lay in the hot pan in a single layer. They should start to caramelise immediately.

2 After about 2 minutes, carefully turn the bananas and caramelise the other side; don't stir more than you need to or you will break them up. Remove the bananas from the pan and set aside. Wipe out the pan with kitchen paper (otherwise the leftover caramel will turn bitter) and caramelise the remaining bananas in the same way. Cool slightly.

3 Put the caramelised bananas and 3 tablespoons liqueur in a food processor or blender and whizz to a purée. Transfer to a bowl and cool.

4 Make the bavarois base and set aside to cool.

5 Beat the banana purée into the bavarois base, adding an extra 1–2 tablespoons liqueur to taste, if liked. Chill until the mixture starts to set around the sides. At this stage, whip the cream until softly stiff and fold into the bavarois using a large metal spoon. Pour into lightly oiled individual moulds or one large bowl and chill until set.

SERVES 8–10

4 large, ripe bananas

70g caster sugar

3–5 tablespoons crème de banane or Baileys liqueur, to taste

1 quantity Bavarois base (page 92)

200ml double cream

FOR A DECADENT DESSERT, SERVE WITH CARAMEL BANANAS IN RUM SYRUP (PAGE 24) AS ILLUSTRATED

Espresso coffee and roasted almond bavarois

You need a large shot of good strong coffee for this. Either make it yourself or buy a double strength espresso from a good takeaway!

1 Make the bavarois base and cool.

2 Preheat the oven to 180°C, Gas 4. Spread the almond flakes out on a baking tray and toast in the oven for about 10 minutes, until nicely browned; watch carefully as they burn quite quickly. Tip the nuts on to a plate to cool, then grind them to a fine powder. (A coffee grinder is ideal for this.)

3 Stir the espresso coffee into the bavarois base, cover and chill.

4 Once the bavarois mixture starts to set at the edges, whip the cream in a bowl until softly stiff. Fold the almonds into the coffee bavarois, then fold in the cream. Spoon into lightly oiled individual moulds or one large bowl and return to the fridge to set.

SERVES 8–10

1 quantity Bavarois base (page 92)

150g flaked almonds

100ml strong espresso coffee, cooled

200ml double cream

ACCOMPANY WITH LANGUES DE CHAT (PAGE 173) OR BABY MERINGUES (PAGE 179)

SOUFFLES

Hot soufflés are simply a base of crème pâtissière combined with a flavouring mixture – such as fruit purée, melted chocolate or praline – folded together with French meringue. The mixture is spooned into prepared ramekins or a larger soufflé dish and baked at once to towering triumphs. Hot soufflés stay aloft for only a minute or two so you must serve them fast. For convenience you can prepare the crème pâtissière base and flavouring mixture ahead and keep them chilled.

Hot soufflés rely on the magic of culinary physics. Whisked air is held in tiny air bubbles formed within egg white protein. When heat is applied, the hot air expands inside the tiny bubbles and the protein sets around each air bubble. As the soufflé cools, the air contracts and seeps out, so the soufflé sinks gracefully. A moderate oven temperature is essential to allow time for the air to rise before the protein sets.

Preparing a soufflé dish

To ensure the soufflé mixture can 'climb' up the sides of the dish, you first need to brush the insides with soft butter, then a fine crumb mixture. If the dish isn't prepared properly, the soufflé may not rise evenly.

1 Using a pastry brush, apply a generous layer of soft butter using vertical strokes. Chill until set.
2 Brush with a second layer of butter in the same way just before applying the coating.
3 For the coating, use 4–6 tablespoons ground almonds or hazelnuts (toasted if preferred), or grated dark chocolate, depending on the recipe. Tip it into the dish and rotate to ensure the sides (and base) are evenly and liberally coated.

Note: Each of the following recipes makes six individual soufflés in 150ml dishes; or eight smaller soufflés in 120ml ramekins.

Crème pâtissière base

This base is very thick, almost the consistency of choux paste. It must be both cooked thoroughly and perfectly smooth when you incorporate it into the soufflé mixture.

1 Heat the milk and cream in a heavy-based saucepan with 1 tablespoon of the sugar until it starts to scald. Meanwhile, sift the flour and cornflour together.

2 Beat the egg yolks and remaining sugar together in a large bowl, then beat in the flour, a third at a time.

3 Slowly pour on a third of the hot creamy milk, whisking well so the mixture remains smooth. Whisk this back into the pan.

4 Simmer gently, whisking continuously, for about 3–4 minutes until smooth and thickened. Transfer to a bowl, cover and cool, stirring occasionally to stop a skin forming.

MAKES ABOUT 320ml
150ml milk
100ml double cream
40g caster sugar
15g plain flour
10g cornflour
3 large free-range egg yolks

Orange and lemon soufflés

This is light and refreshing — a perfect way to end a rich winter dinner. Make up the crème pâtissière base in advance, folding in the meringue just before baking. Use either freshly squeezed or bought orange juice – as long as this is fresh and not concentrated. As the mixture is light and delicate, it is more suited to individual soufflés than a large one.

1 Prepare the crème pâtissière base and mix in the citrus zests. Pour the lemon juice and all of the orange juice into a saucepan and boil until reduced to 200ml. Stir into the crème pâtissière and set aside to cool. Mix in the Grand Marnier.

2 Meanwhile, coat the individual soufflé dishes or ramekins with two layers of melted butter, then ground nuts or grated chocolate (see left). Preheat the oven to 190°C, Gas 5.

3 When almost ready to serve, whisk the egg whites in a bowl until they form firm peaks, then gradually whisk in the sugar. Carefully fold this meringue into the citrus mixture and spoon into the prepared dishes. Level the tops with a palette knife or the back of a spoon. Place on a baking tray and bake until risen and golden, allowing 12–15 minutes for small ramekins; 15–18 minutes for larger individual dishes.

4 Slide the soufflé dishes on to dessert plates if required. Serve at once.

SERVES 6–8
1 quantity Crème pâtissière base (see above)
grated zest and juice of 1 large lemon
grated zest of 1 large orange
500ml fresh orange juice
3 tablespoons Grand Marnier
2 large free-range egg whites
50g caster sugar
TO COAT THE DISHES:
40g unsalted butter, melted
4–6 tablespoons ground almonds or hazelnuts, or grated dark chocolate

Rhubarb and vanilla soufflé

SERVES 6–8

500g tender pink rhubarb

2 tablespoons water (optional)

1 vanilla pod

100g caster sugar

1 quantity Crème pâtissière base (page 99)

2 large free-range egg whites

TO COAT THE DISHES:

40g unsalted butter, melted

4–6 tablespoons ground almonds or hazelnuts, or grated dark chocolate

TO FINISH (OPTIONAL):

icing sugar, to dust

SERVE A SCOOP OF VANILLA OR GINGER ICE CREAM (PAGES 57–8) OR FROMAGE FRAIS SORBET (PAGE 76) IN A SMALL DISH ALONGSIDE THE SOUFFLE, IF YOU LIKE

Buy tender, pink 'forced' rhubarb for this dessert. This is at its best from December through to early March, though you may still find it in the shops in early summer, and again from late autumn.

1 Trim the rhubarb and cut into small chunks. Wash if necessary and shake dry. Place in a saucepan, adding the 2 tablespoons water if you didn't need to wash the fruit.

2 Add the vanilla pod and half of the sugar. Heat slowly, stirring until the sugar dissolves. Cover and simmer for about 5 minutes until the fruit has softened. Tip into a fine sieve placed over a bowl to drain off excess juice.

3 Return this juice to the pan, adding the vanilla pod. Boil until reduced by half to intensify the flavour, then stir back into the rhubarb. Discard the vanilla pod.

4 Tip the fruit into a food processor or blender and whizz to a smooth purée. Transfer to a bowl and set aside to cool.

5 Make the crème pâtissière base and cool.

6 Meanwhile, coat individual dishes or a 1 litre soufflé dish with two layers of melted butter, then ground nuts or grated chocolate (see page 98). Preheat the oven to 190°C, Gas 5.

7 Mix the rhubarb purée into the crème pâtissière. Now whisk the egg whites in a large clean bowl until they form firm peaks. Gradually whisk in the remaining caster sugar until you have a glossy meringue. Fold this into the rhubarb mixture.

8 Immediately divide between the prepared ramekins, or spoon into the large soufflé dish and level with a palette knife or the back of a spoon. Stand on a baking tray and bake until risen and golden. Allow 12–15 minutes for small ramekins; 15–18 minutes for larger individual dishes; 25–30 minutes for one large soufflé. If you have time, dust quickly with icing sugar. Serve immediately.

Spiced quince soufflé

You can find perfumed golden quince from around the end of September – Greek delis are a good source of supply. An old kitchen garden fruit, they look like plump, over-sized pears and indeed you can substitute firm pears when quince are out of season. Quince flesh is hard and not for eating raw. I like to poach it in a light sugar syrup flavoured with Chinese style spices – it turns a delicate rose pink colour with a heavenly fragrance. For this recipe, the poached quince flesh is then puréed.

1 Peel the quince thinly, using a swivel vegetable peeler. Cut into quarters (you will need to use a heavy cook's knife) and remove the cores. Chop the flesh into small cubes and place in a saucepan with the stock syrup.

2 Stir in the spices and orange zest, bring to the boil, then cover and simmer gently for about 15 minutes until soft. Drain the fruit and discard the whole spices (save the syrup, as it can be used again). Purée the quince flesh in a blender or food processor until smooth. You should have approximately 300ml purée. Transfer to a bowl and cool, then cover and chill.

3 Make the crème pâtissière base and cool.

4 Meanwhile, coat individual dishes or a 1 litre soufflé dish with two layers of melted butter, then ground nuts (see page 98). Preheat the oven to 190ºC, Gas 5.

5 Beat the quince purée into the crème pâtissière. Whisk the egg whites to firm peaks in a large clean bowl. Gradually whisk in the sugar, then fold the meringue into the creamy fruit mixture.

6 Divide between the ramekins, or spoon into the large soufflé dish and level with a palette knife or back of a spoon. Stand on a baking tray and bake until risen and golden brown. Allow 12–15 minutes for small ramekins; 15–18 minutes for larger individual dishes; 25–30 minutes for one large soufflé.

7 If you feel so inclined you could dust the tops with icing sugar as soon as they emerge from the oven. Serve instantly.

SERVES 6–8

500g quince (about 1 large one)

300ml Stock syrup (page 200)

2 star anise

1 large cinnamon stick

½ teaspoon Chinese five-spice powder

2 strips of orange zest

1 quantity Crème pâtissière base (page 99)

2 large free-range egg whites

2 tablespoons caster sugar

TO COAT THE DISHES:

40g unsalted butter, melted

4–6 tablespoons finely chopped almonds or hazelnuts

TO FINISH (OPTIONAL):

icing sugar, to dust

Little white chocolate and kahlua soufflés

These little soufflés look very appealing with their cocoa-dusted tops. Effectively they are based on a white chocolate crème pâtissière, which works best as individual soufflés. I like to bake the mixture over a layer of marinated cherries and serve the soufflés with a warm Plum coulis (page 11). You simply spoon the coulis into the centre of the hot soufflés as you serve them.

1 Break up the white chocolate and place in a large bowl. Heat the milk until boiling, then slowly pour on to the chocolate, stirring until melted.
2 Sift the cornflour and flour together. Beat the egg yolks and 50g of the sugar together in a bowl, then mix in the flours, beating until smooth.
3 Slowly pour on the hot chocolate milk, stirring briskly. Return to the saucepan and stir over a gentle heat until thickened and smooth. Simmer for about 30 seconds, then remove from the heat.
4 Meanwhile, boil the coffee liqueur in a small pan until reduced by about half. Stir into the chocolate crème pâtissière. Cool.
5 Coat the individual soufflé dishes with two layers of melted butter, then grated chocolate or ground nuts (page 98). If using cherries, divide them between the dishes. Preheat the oven to 190°C, Gas 5.
6 Beat the cream into the chilled chocolate mixture to loosen it a little. Whisk the egg whites in a clean bowl until they stand in peaks, then gradually whisk in the remaining 25g sugar. Fold this meringue into the chocolate crème pâtissière.
7 Divide between the prepared dishes and level the tops with a palette knife or back of a spoon. Place on a baking tray and bake for 15–18 minutes until risen and golden brown. Dust the tops with cocoa as you take the soufflés from the oven and serve instantly.

SERVES 6
150g white chocolate
250ml milk
10g cornflour
15g plain flour
3 large free-range eggs, separated
75g caster sugar
100ml Kahlua or Tia Maria liqueur
6 tablespoons Marinated cherries (page 13), or
   bottled dark red cherries, drained (optional)
4 tablespoons double cream
TO COAT THE DISHES:
40g unsalted butter, melted
4–6 tablespoons grated dark chocolate, or
   ground almonds or hazelnuts
TO FINISH (OPTIONAL):
cocoa powder, to dust

crêpes and batters

Crêpes

This is the most basic of batters, which you can vary to taste. Using 2 eggs rather than one gives you a richer batter. Incorporating the yolks and whisked whites separately into the batter – as for soufflé crêpes (below) – gives you a lighter batter. You can also add flavourings to the batter, such as ground sweet spices or roasted chopped almonds. Hazelnut and chocolate spread (Nutella) is one of my favourites – beat in 2 tablespoons for scrumptious chocolate crêpes.

1 Place the flour and salt in a food processor and add the egg(s), butter and half of the milk. Whizz until smooth and creamy, scraping down the sides once or twice to dislodge any lumps or stray pockets of flour. With the motor running, mix in the remaining milk.

2 Leave the batter to rest for 30 minutes if you like, although this is no longer deemed to be necessary as flours are now so thoroughly refined.

3 Cook your crêpes (according to the instructions overleaf), stirring the batter occasionally. You should get about 12–16 if you make thin ones, approximately 20cm in diameter. Add your choice of filling and cream, ice cream or sauce and serve.

Soufflé crêpes

To make these light crêpes, you need the above quantities of ingredients, including 2 eggs. Separate the eggs and whizz the yolks with the other batter ingredients. Before cooking, whisk the egg whites until softly stiff, then fold into the batter with a metal spoon. Cook as normal crêpes, but handle them gently so as not to knock out the air.

CREPE FILLINGS For a simple dessert, spread cooked crêpes with homemade strawberry jam, roll up and top with a dollop of Crème chantilly (page 50).

For a special pudding, the possibilities are endless. You can use a filling of sliced fruit or berry fruits, such as peach or strawberry slices, fresh raspberries or blueberries – or a mixture of fresh fruit. Roasted fruits also make delectable crêpe fillings – the best are apples, pears, white peaches, plums and pineapple (see pages 34–43). You can combine these with any of the flavoured creams (on pages 51–2).

For sheer indulgence, serve with a crêpe sauce (page 110), plus a trickle of pouring cream, a dollop of Crème chantilly or lemon grass flavoured crème fraîche (page 50), or a scoop of homemade ice cream (pages 57–63).

MAKES 12–16 CREPES

125g plain flour
2 good pinches of salt
1 or 2 medium free-range eggs
1 tablespoon melted butter
300ml milk
sunflower oil, to grease the pan

FILL CREPES WITH A MEDLEY OF SUMMER BERRIES AND SERVE ACCOMPANIED BY POURING CREAM

COOKING CREPES

Cooking crêpes at the correct, constant temperature is the main secret of success. You achieve this with a good pan – one with a heavy base and good heat retention. Cast-iron and heavy-gauge anodised aluminium pans are considered the most suitable. A non-stick coating makes for easier cooking especially first time round, but if you season a good uncoated crêpe pan and never clean it with a metal scourer then it will build up a natural patina that lasts years. A poor quality non-stick pan, on the other hand, will lose its virtues over time. A proper crêpe pan will have short sloping sides so the crêpe can just slip out. It should be 20–23cm in diameter.

To season a new crêpe pan
To season a new traditional iron or aluminium pan, first wash and dry it well. Then place the empty pan on a medium-low heat and heat up slowly for about 10 minutes until you can feel a strong heat rising and see a heat haze. Remove and carefully wipe it with a wad of kitchen paper that has been dipped in a bland vegetable oil. Make sure the surface is well coated in oil, then wipe it again with a clean wad of kitchen paper. Now you can start to cook your first crêpe.

To cook crêpes

1 Pour the batter into a jug and have a small ladle at the ready. Most crêpes are best made with about 2–3 tablespoons (30–45ml) of batter. Pour a small amount of bland sunflower oil or light olive oil into a cup. Start to heat the empty 20–23cm crêpe pan until you can feel a good heat rising. Add a few drops of oil, tilt to grease the base of the pan, then tip out any excess.

2 Pour in about 2–3 tablespoons of batter from the ladle.

3 Immediately swirl the pan so the batter coats the entire base thinly. (Any excess runny batter can be tipped back into the jug.) Quickly put the pan back on the heat and cook until the batter is set and little holes appear in the surface, about 1½ minutes.

4 Slip a palette knife under the crêpe, then flip it over. Cook the other side for about 30 seconds.

5 Slide the cooked crêpe out on to a clean tea towel placed on a wire rack. Repeat to cook the rest of the batter. After a while you won't need to grease the pan every time. Stack the crêpes on top of each other as they are cooked and keep them wrapped in the tea towel.

6 If serving shortly, keep the crêpes warm in a warming oven until ready to serve. If you are making them well ahead, it's better to wrap them in a double layer of cling film or a large food bag to stop them drying out, then reheat in the oven, loosely wrapped in foil, at 180°C, Gas 4 for 10–15 minutes to serve.

SAUCES FOR CREPES

Crème chantilly (page 50) is the classic crêpe accompaniment, but there are lots of sauces that go well with crêpes, including Chocolate sauce (page 131). The following are especially good.

Caramel sauce

MAKES ABOUT 350ml

250g caster sugar

3 tablespoons water

125ml double cream

2 tablespoons sweetened condensed milk

75g butter

Nice with crêpes and ice cream, this is also good with tarte tatins and sponge puddings. It keeps for a week in a screw-topped jar in the fridge, but you will need to reheat it gently to serve.

1 Melt the sugar with the water in a heavy-based saucepan over a very low heat. This takes up to 10 minutes – you might find it helpful to swirl the pan once or twice. Meanwhile, fill the sink with cold water.

2 When the syrup is clear, raise the heat and cook to a mid-caramel colour. Don't let it become dark or it will be bitter. As soon as it's ready, dunk the base of the pan in cold water for a minute or two to cool.

3 Place the pan on a heatproof surface, add the remaining ingredients and beat until smooth. Serve warm.

Orange and lemon sauce

MAKES ABOUT 140ml

250ml fresh orange juice

1 slightly heaped teaspoon cornflour

1 tablespoon water

1 tablespoon lemon juice

1 tablespoon Cointreau

2 teaspoons Stock syrup (page 200) or icing sugar

1 Boil the orange juice in a small saucepan until reduced by half.

2 Meanwhile, mix the cornflour to a smooth paste with the water and add the lemon juice. Off the heat, whisk the cornflour mixture into the hot orange juice.

3 Return to the heat and bring back to a simmer, stirring briskly. Cook for about 30 seconds, then add the Cointreau and stock syrup or icing sugar. Allow to cool a little. Serve warm.

Raspberry melba sauce

MAKES ABOUT 200ml

250g raspberries, preferably slightly overripe

good squeeze of lemon juice

a little icing sugar (optional)

1 tablespoon framboise eau-de-vie (optional)

1 Put the raspberries in a food processor or blender and process to a thin purée. Turn into a sieve over a bowl and rub with the back of a ladle to extract as much juice as possible; discard the seeds.

2 Add the lemon juice and sweeten with a little icing sugar if necessary. Flavour with the framboise if using. Serve at room temperature.

Baby buttermilk pancakes

These are easy to whizz up in a food processor, then cook quickly in a lightly greased frying pan or hot griddle. Buttermilk gives the batter a light tangy flavour; it's available from many supermarkets and healthfood shops. I like to serve these little pancakes with roasted plums or figs and scoops of ice cream or whipped Crème chantilly (page 50), plus trickles of maple syrup.

1 Put the flour, salt, baking powder, bicarbonate of soda, sugar and vanilla seeds into a food processor and pulse briefly to blend.
2 Add the egg yolks, melted butter, buttermilk and milk. Whizz to a smooth batter, scraping down the sides of the bowl once or twice. Transfer to a bowl.
3 Whisk the egg whites in a separate bowl to soft floppy peaks, then fold into the batter.
4 Heat a griddle pan or heavy-based frying pan until you can feel a good heat rising, then lightly oil the pan.
5 Using a small ladle, pour in about 1–2 tablespoons of batter to make a pancake about 10cm in diameter. Repeat to shape about 4 pancakes in the pan, depending on its size. Cook for a minute or so until the tops are set and little holes appear in the surface.
6 Flip the pancakes over and brown lightly on the other side, then transfer to a tea towel placed on a wire rack. Repeat with the remaining batter, stacking the pancakes as they are cooked. Serve warm.

SERVES 4
175g plain flour
½ teaspoon fine sea salt
½ teaspoon baking powder
½ teaspoon bicarbonate of soda
1 tablespoon caster sugar
seeds from 1 vanilla pod
2 medium free-range eggs, separated
15g butter, melted and cooled
200ml buttermilk
100ml milk
a little sunflower oil, to cook

DELICIOUS WITH ROASTED PLUMS (PAGE 41) OR ROASTED BLACK FIGS WITH SPICED BALSAMIC SYRUP (PAGE 42), PLUS WHIPPED CREME CHANTILLY (PAGE 50) AND DRIZZLES OF MAPLE SYRUP

Classic crêpes suzette

SERVES 4

1 quantity Crêpe batter (page 107)
6 large oranges
50g demerara sugar
about 90–100ml Grand Marnier
sunflower oil, to grease the pan
knob of unsalted butter, to cook

For these, you simply flavour the basic crêpe batter with grated orange zest and bathe the cooked crêpes in a warm, tangy orange sauce spiked with Grand Marnier. This isn't a dessert for a large party – up to 4 servings is manageable.

1 Make the crêpe batter. Finely grate the zest from 2 oranges and stir into the batter.

2 For the sauce, finely pare the zest from a further 2 oranges, using a swivel vegetable peeler, and cut into fine julienne strips. Blanch these in boiling water for 1 minute, then drain and pat dry; set aside. Squeeze the juice from 3 oranges and strain to remove pips. Peel and segment the other 3 oranges, cutting away the peel and pith with a sharp knife, then cutting between the membranes to release the segments (illustrated on page 33). Set aside.

3 Heat the sugar in a heavy-based saucepan over a low heat until melted; avoid stirring but shake the pan a little to encourage the process. Once every grain has dissolved, add the orange zest julienne and simmer for 2 minutes or until the syrup forms a light caramel. Don't let the sugar burn or the sauce will taste bitter.

4 When the sugar syrup starts to caramelise, carefully add the Grand Marnier – it will splutter – and cook for a minute or so to burn off the alcohol.

5 Pour in the orange juice and boil until reduced by half. Remove from the heat, slide in the orange segments and leave to cool and macerate until warm.

6 Meanwhile, cook the crêpes (see page 109) and keep wrapped in a tea towel until required.

7 When ready to serve, melt a little butter in a large frying pan and add a cooked crêpe. Reheat for a few seconds and fold into quarters. Repeat with another one or two crêpes (for one serving). Spoon over a portion of orange sauce, making sure you include some segments and zest julienne. Slide on to a warmed dessert plate. Repeat and repeat, allowing 2–3 crêpes per serving.

Cherry and almond clafoutis

This is based on the classic French favourite. Here an almond-flavoured batter is baked in a shallow pan over a layer of pitted fresh cherries. Prepare the batter and fruits in advance, but put them together and bake the pudding at the last minute. The batter benefits from resting for a full 24 hours. You can either make one large pudding or 6 small ones according to the variation (below).

1 Put the ground almonds, flour, salt and sugar into a food processor and whizz for a few seconds to blend. Add the eggs, egg yolks and cream and blend to a smooth batter, scraping down the sides of the bowl once or twice. Tip into a jug or bowl, cover and refrigerate for 24 hours.

2 In the meantime, stone the cherries and pat them dry if they are particularly juicy. Rub the inside of a large ovenproof sauté pan or gratin dish, about 23–25cm in diameter, with softened butter.

3 Preheat the oven to 190°C, Gas 5. Scatter the cherries over the base of the pan or dish. Stir the batter in the jug, then pour over the cherries. Bake for about 20 minutes until risen and golden brown. The middle may be slightly flatter than the surrounding batter but it should be set. If not, then bake for a little longer.

4 Dust with icing sugar and serve at once.

To make individual clafoutis

Butter six 10cm tartlet tins or Yorkshire pudding tins and divide the cherries between them. Pour on the batter and bake at 200°C, Gas 6 for about 12 minutes.

SERVES 6
50g ground almonds
15g strong plain flour
good pinch of sea salt
100g caster sugar
2 large free-range eggs
3 large free-range egg yolks
250ml double cream
300g ripe fresh cherries, or 250g Marinated cherries (page 13), drained
unsalted butter, softened, to grease pan
icing sugar, sifted, to dust

Fruit tempura

SERVES 4–6

125g rice flour

250ml light beer

300ml cold water

1 large free-range egg yolk

2 large free-range egg whites

4–5 different pieces of fruits (choose from firm ripe pear, dessert apple, banana, plums, apricots, ½ small pineapple)

juice of 1 lemon

sunflower oil, for deep-frying

icing sugar, sifted, to dust

vanilla sugar (page 129), to dust

SMALL SCOOPS OF VANILLA ICE CREAM (PAGE 57) ARE AN APPROPRIATE ACCOMPANIMENT

To give fruit fritters a new twist, we now use rice flour for our light Oriental style batters. The trick is to draw the slices of fruit quickly through the batter so they have a light – even partial – covering, rather than immerse them for a generous coating. A light beer gives the batter a tasty hint of yeast. Use a fat or sugar thermometer to keep a check on the temperature of the oil.

1 For the batter, put the rice flour into a large bowl. Add the beer and water and beat using a large balloon whisk until smooth. Then beat in the egg yolk.

2 Prepare the fruits. Peel, halve and core the pear and/or apple, then cut into ½cm thick slices. Halve the banana lengthways, then cut each piece in two. Toss these fruits in lemon juice to prevent discoloration. Quarter plums and apricots, discarding the stones. Peel the pineapple and cut into 1cm thick slices; halve the slices and remove the core. You should have enough for 5–7 pieces of fruit per serving.

3 When ready to serve, whisk the egg whites in a bowl until softly stiff and fold into the batter, using a large metal spoon. One-third fill a fairly deep, heavy saucepan with sunflower oil and heat to a temperature of 180°C.

4 Pick up a piece of fruit and dust it lightly with icing sugar, then draw it quickly through the batter to coat lightly and place in the hot oil. Quickly repeat with 2 more fruit pieces. Fry for about 2 minutes until golden brown and crisp. Remove and drain on kitchen paper.

5 Cook the remaining fruit in the same way, in similar small batches. Only dip the fruits in the batter as you are ready to fry them. Also, make sure the oil remains at 180°C; if it drops below, hold back on the frying until it returns to this temperature. Keep the tempura warm on a baking tray, uncovered in a low oven until you have cooked them all.

6 Serve the tempura as soon as possible, while they are hot and crunchy. Dust lightly with vanilla sugar.

Lemon and honey rum babas

Babas are individual rich yeast cakes baked in little ring moulds (sometimes sold as ring do-nut moulds) and soaked in a rum-flavoured syrup. They are delicious served with glazed apricots and crème chantilly. You might like to add a sprinkling of chopped pistachios too.

1 Sift the flour and salt into a large bowl. Finely crumble in the fresh yeast if using, or add the dried yeast. Scatter in the lemon zest and stir to mix.

2 Warm the honey a little, until runny but not hot. In a bowl, beat together the honey, vanilla extract and 3 eggs.

3 Add the honey mixture to the flour with the 100g butter and beat thoroughly, using an electric mixer, for about 3 minutes until smooth.

4 Beat the remaining eggs lightly, then gradually work into the dough, with the mixer on medium speed; this should take a good 5 minutes. Add the sultanas with the final addition of egg.

5 Cover the bowl and leave the dough to rise in a warm place, such as an airing cupboard, until doubled in size. As the dough is quite rich this may take several hours, but check every 30 minutes or so.

6 Liberally grease 6 baba moulds or little ring moulds with soft butter. Gently knock back the risen dough and divide into 6 pieces. Place in the moulds, cover loosely with lightly greased cling film and leave in a warm place for about 30 minutes until the dough has risen to three-quarters fill the tins.

7 Preheat the oven to 190°C, Gas 5. Remove the cling film cover and stand the baba tins on a baking sheet. Bake for about 20 minutes until golden brown and firm, but springy when lightly pressed. Leave in the tins for 5 minutes, then turn out on to a wire rack, loosening the sides with a table knife. Cool until tepid.

8 Prick the tops and sides of the babas with a fine skewer, then return to the moulds. Mix the rum into the hot stock syrup and slowly pour over the babas to soak them thoroughly.

9 Once all the syrup has been absorbed, turn out the babas on to plates and chill until required. To serve, fill with glazed apricots and top each rum baba with a quenelle of crème chantilly. Serve the rest of the apricots alongside, drizzled with any remaining syrup.

SERVES 6

250g plain flour

1 teaspoon fine sea salt

15g fresh yeast, or 1 sachet easy-blend dried yeast

grated zest of 1 lemon

2 scant tablespoons clear honey

1 teaspoon vanilla extract

6 medium free-range eggs

100g unsalted butter, softened until almost runny, plus extra to grease the mould

75g sultanas

250ml hot Stock syrup (page 200)

90ml white rum

TO SERVE:

Glazed apricots (page 43)

Crème chantilly (page 50)

PILE GLAZED APRICOTS INTO RUM BABAS AND TOP WITH QUENELLES OF CREME CHANTILLY FOR AN EYE-CATCHING DESSERT

homely puddings

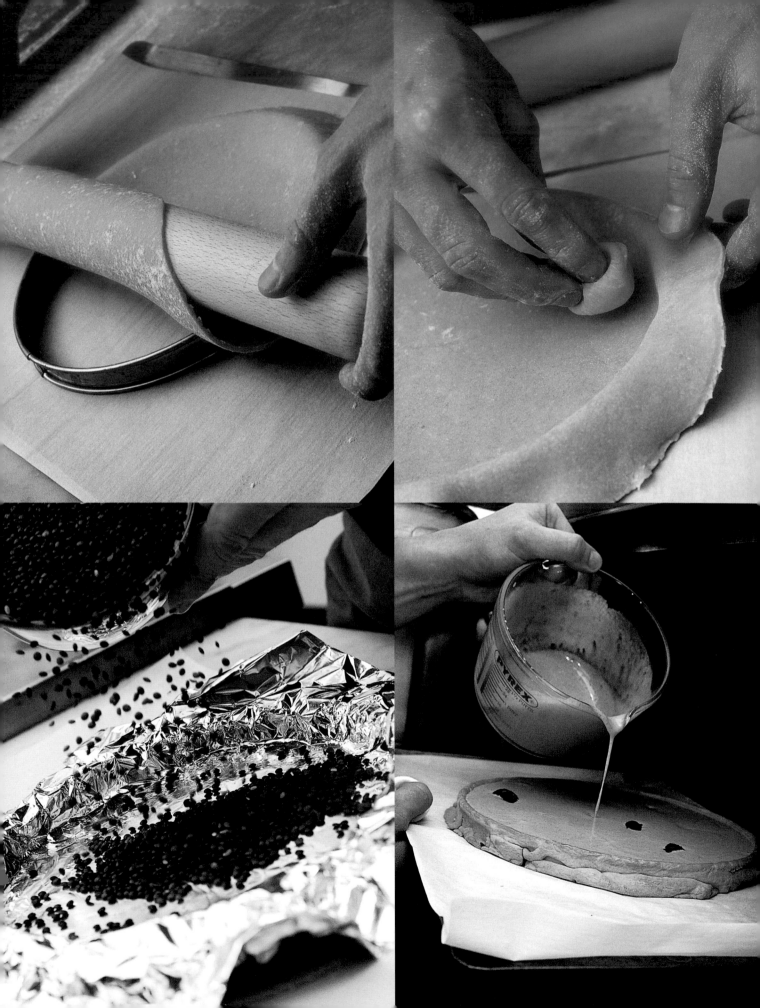

Prune and Armagnac custard tart

A velvety smooth custard tart enriched with prunes macerated in Armagnac. It really doesn't need any embellishment, except perhaps a scoop of ice cream. A great pudding to round off Sunday lunch.

1 Put the prunes and tea in a saucepan, bring to the boil and simmer for 1 minute. Set aside to cool for 30 minutes. Drain and stone the prunes, then place in a bowl. Stir in the Armagnac and leave to macerate.

2 Roll out the pastry thinly on a surface lightly dusted with flour. Using the rolling pin, lift it over a 24cm flan ring, 3–3.5cm deep, placed on a baking sheet lined with baking parchment (or flan tin of the same dimensions with removable base).

3 Press the pastry into the corners, using a small ball of dough (rather than fingers which could tear the pastry). Leave the edge overhanging.

4 Line the pastry case with foil, pressing it into the corners, and fill with baking beans. (Note, you do not prick the base or the liquid filling might seep out.) Chill the pastry case for 20 minutes. Preheat the oven to 190°C, Gas 5.

5 Meanwhile, put the milk and cream in a saucepan with the lemon zest. Slit the vanilla pod and scrape out the seeds with the tip of a knife, adding them to the pan with the empty pod. Heat slowly until on the point of boiling, then take off the heat, stir in the sugar and set aside to infuse for 30 minutes.

6 Bake the pastry case blind for 15 minutes. Remove from the oven and lower the setting to 150°C, Gas 2. Carefully remove the foil and baking beans from the flan case.

7 Cut two thirds of the prunes into small chunks and scatter over the pastry base. Beat the egg yolks and whole eggs together in a bowl. Remove the lemon zest and vanilla pod from the creamy milk. Bring back to the boil, then slowly pour on to the beaten eggs, whisking.

8 Put the remaining prunes into a food processor and whizz lightly to a pulp. Then with the motor running, slowly pour in the custard through the feeder tube, processing until evenly blended. Pass through a sieve into a jug, rubbing with the back of a ladle.

9 Return the pastry case to the oven, pulling the shelf out as far as it is safe. Slowly pour in the prune custard – it should come almost to the top. Very carefully push the oven shelf back and bake the tart for 50 minutes to 1 hour, until the custard barely wobbles when shaken.

10 With a sharp knife at an angle, trim the pastry level with the top of the flan ring (see right). Cool until tepid, then carefully unmould the tart and slide on to a large flat plate. Serve at room temperature.

SERVES 6

200g mi-cuit (no-need-to-soak) Agen prunes
about 200ml weak Earl Grey tea
3 tablespoons Armagnac
1 quantity Pâte sucrée (page 202)
400ml milk
200ml double cream
3 strips of lemon zest
1 vanilla pod
75g caster sugar
2 large free-range egg yolks
2 large free-range eggs

EQUALLY DELICIOUS SERVED ALONE OR TOPPED WITH A SCOOP OF VANILLA ICE CREAM (PAGE 57)

Orange curd layer pudding

This delightful old-fashioned pudding cooks to a delicious light soufflé sponge on top, with a thick zingy curd sauce underneath. It looks like a nightmare just before you bake it, all runny and slightly lumpy – the transformation is little short of a miracle. I wonder whoever first thought of such a recipe, or was it a happy accident? Bake it in a heatproof glass dish to reveal the appealing layers – I use a Bodum glass soufflé dish. For a dinner party, add a splash of Grand Marnier or Cointreau.

1 Put the orange and lemon juices in a saucepan, bring to the boil and boil until reduced by just over half – to 150ml. Set aside to cool and then stir in the liqueur, if using.

2 Butter the sides of a 1 litre soufflé dish, or other similar ovenproof dish. Preheat the oven to 180°C, Gas 4.

3 In a mixing bowl, beat the butter with the sugar and lemon zest until soft and creamy. Beat in the egg yolks, one at a time. Sift the flour and baking powder together over the mixture, then beat in.

4 Slowly add the orange juice and milk to the mixture, stirring to blend. Do not worry if the mixture looks curdled or lumpy at this stage. It will be fine. Trust me – I'm a chef.

5 Now whisk the egg whites in another bowl until they form softly stiff peaks. Beat a third of the whisked egg whites into the runny cake mixture, then carefully fold in the rest using a large metal spoon and a figure-of-eight motion.

6 Stand the prepared dish in a roasting tin, then pour in the mixture. Surround the dish with boiling water to create a bain-marie and place in the oven. Bake for 1–1¼ hours until the pudding is golden brown and firm on top, and creamy underneath. Reduce the oven temperature slightly towards the end of cooking if the top appears to be browning too quickly.

7 Remove the dish from the bain-marie and leave to stand for 10 minutes or a little longer. Dust the pudding with icing sugar before serving. As you spoon it out, make sure you get right down to the bottom to include some of the soft curd layer. There's no need for cream, unless you really must.

SERVES 4–6

300ml fresh orange juice

grated zest and juice of 1 lemon

3 tablespoons Grand Marnier or Cointreau (optional)

60g butter, softened, plus extra to grease dish

100g caster sugar

4 large free-range eggs, separated

60g self-raising flour

½ teaspoon baking powder

150ml milk

icing sugar, to dust

Baguette and butter pudding laced with Baileys

SERVES 6

50g butter, softened

½ large French stick (about 150g), thinly sliced

60g sultanas or dried cranberries, or a mixture
   of both

2 large free-range egg yolks

2 large free-range eggs

40g caster sugar

300ml double cream

300ml milk

4 tablespoons Baileys cream liqueur, or more
   to taste

demerara sugar, to sprinkle

3 tablespoons apricot jam

Most chefs now seem to have their own version of bread and butter pudding, using rich breads such as panettone, pain au chocolat and brioche. I like to use thin slices of French bread or croissants – these allow the richness of the eggy custard to come through. A good splash of Baileys cream liqueur takes this into the ethereal. Serve the pudding warm, not piping hot, trickled with a little more Baileys if that's not too much of an overkill.

1 Use a large knob of the butter to grease the sides of a 1.5 litre shallow ovenproof dish. Spread the bread slices with the remaining butter. Arrange the bread in the dish in overlapping layers, sprinkling the dried fruit in between.

2 Beat the egg yolks, whole eggs and sugar together in a large bowl until creamy, then beat in the cream, milk and Baileys. Slowly pour this mixture over the bread.

3 Press the bread slices down gently with your fingers so they are completely submerged.

4 Leave to stand for about 20 minutes to allow the bread to soak up the custard. Preheat the oven to 180°C, Gas 4.

5 Stand the dish in a roasting tin and surround with boiling water to come halfway up the sides of the dish. (A bain-marie is used to avoid overheating the custard, which otherwise might curdle.) Sprinkle with demerara sugar and bake for 40–50 minutes until golden. Shortly before this time is up, warm the apricot jam until runny.

6 Dab this glaze over the surface of the pudding and leave to stand for 15 minutes before serving. The custard will continue to cook and firm up during this time. Trickle a little more Baileys over each portion to serve if you like.

Roasted rhubarb and apple crumble

Crumbles can be heavy, stodgy puddings. This is an altogether lighter affair, made in an ovenproof sauté pan. The filling is caramelised yet sharp and fruity, and the fudgey topping is scattered on loosely so it bakes to a crisp crunch. Many other fruits and spices complement rhubarb, including apple, vanilla and nutmeg.

1 Preheat the oven to 190°C, Gas 5. Trim off the ends of the rhubarb, then cut into chunks about 5cm long. Wash if necessary and pat dry in a clean tea towel. Quarter, core and thinly peel the apple. Cut into chunks, about 2cm in size.

2 Heat an enamelled cast-iron or other heavy-based sauté pan until very hot; it should almost start to smoke.

3 Toss the rhubarb and apple in the vanilla sugar, then tip into the pan and spread out to a single layer. The fruit will start to caramelise almost immediately if the pan is at the right temperature. Leave for a couple of minutes, then turn with a thin metal spoon or spatula so the fruit stays intact as far as possible; it shouldn't become too mushy.

4 Continue cooking for a further 3–5 minutes until the pieces feel just tender when pierced with the tip of a knife. Remove from the heat and leave to cool slightly while you make the topping.

5 Put the flour and butter in a food processor and process briefly until the mixture resembles fine crumbs. Add the muscovado sugar and whizz for a few seconds more. Grate the nutmeg straight into the mixture, add the oats and blend again briefly.

6 Scatter the topping over the fruit – don't pat it down or level it. Bake the pudding for 20 minutes until the topping is nicely browned. Leave to stand for 10 minutes before serving.

SERVES 4

500g pink tender rhubarb

1 large Braeburn apple

100g vanilla sugar (see below)

TOPPING:

100g plain flour

50g butter, chilled and cut into small cubes

50g light muscovado sugar

freshly grated nutmeg, to taste

40g porridge oats

SERVE WITH CREME ANGLAISE (PAGE 193), CREME FRAICHE OR A SCOOP OF VANILLA OR GINGER ICE CREAM (PAGES 57–8)

VANILLA SUGAR Simply bury 3 vanilla pods in a jar containing about 500g caster sugar. Within a couple of days you will have fragrant vanilla sugar. We find this a good use for split pods that have had their seeds extracted – they still impart lots of flavour.

Steamed toffee, banana and pecan pudding

SERVES 4–6

TOPPING:

50g butter, softened

50g light muscovado sugar

50g pecan halves

PUDDING:

1 large ripe banana

3 ripe passion fruit, or 1 lemon

125g butter, softened

125g caster sugar

3 medium free-range eggs

100g self-raising flour

¼ teaspoon fine sea salt

½ teaspoon baking powder

75g fresh white breadcrumbs

SERVE WITH CREME ANGLAISE (PAGE 193), CREAM, OR MY EASY TOFFEE SAUCE

To my mind this is the ultimate comfort pudding and it is so easy to whizz up in a mixer. For a light texture, I use half breadcrumbs and half flour.

1 Lightly grease a 1 litre heatproof pudding basin. To make the topping, cream the butter and muscovado sugar together in the basin until nicely blended, then spread it around the base and a third of the way up the sides. Press 6 pecan halves down into the topping in a circle. Chop the rest of the nuts and reserve.

2 Mash the banana to a pulp. If using passion fruit, halve and scrape out the pulp into a sieve over a bowl. Rub through to extract the juice; discard the seeds. If using lemon, grate the zest and squeeze the juice.

3 Put the butter, caster sugar, eggs, flour, salt, baking powder and passion fruit juice (or lemon juice and zest) in a food processor or mixer. Whizz until smooth and creamy, scraping down the sides once or twice.

4 Add the banana pulp, chopped pecans and breadcrumbs and pulse lightly until just incorporated.

5 Spoon the mixture into the pudding basin. For the cover, lay a large piece of greaseproof paper on a sheet of foil and pleat them together in the centre (to allow for the pudding to rise). Place over the basin and secure tightly under the rim with kitchen string or a strong rubber band.

6 Place in a steamer over boiling water, or in a large saucepan containing enough boiling water to come halfway up the sides of the basin. Steam for 2 hours, checking the water level every 30 minutes or so and topping up with boiling water as necessary.

7 Lift the basin out of the pan and leave the pudding to stand for 10 minutes. Remove the cover and run a table knife around the side of the pudding. Unmould on to a warm plate to serve.

Easy toffee sauce

300ml double cream

170g light muscovado sugar

4 tablespoons liquid glucose

70g unsalted butter

1 Put half the cream in a heavy-based saucepan. Add the sugar, glucose and butter and slowly bring to the boil, stirring. Once the sugar is dissolved, raise the heat and boil for about 10 minutes, to a light toffee colour, stirring once or twice so it doesn't burn on the base of the pan.

2 Immediately remove from the heat and cool, stirring occasionally to prevent a skin forming. When cold, beat in the remaining cream. Serve at room temperature. If prepared ahead and chilled, then take out of the fridge a good hour before serving. The sauce should be runny.

Steamed chocolate pudding

This scrumptious variation of my steamed toffee pudding is for all chocoholics. Again, it is simple to make – the only tricky part is remembering to top up the pan with boiling water. I like to serve this rich pudding with a white chocolate sauce (see below) or pouring cream.

1 Lightly grease a 1 litre heatproof pudding basin. Cream the sugar and butter for the topping together in the basin, then spread the mixture over the base and a third of the way up the sides.

2 Whizz the pudding ingredients, except the breadcrumbs, in a food processor or mixer until smooth. Add the breadcrumbs and pulse lightly until just incorporated.

3 Spoon the mixture into the pudding basin. Cover with greaseproof paper and foil, pleated together in the centre (to allow room for the pudding to rise), and secure under the rim with kitchen string or a strong rubber band.

4 Steam the pudding for 2 hours, using a steamer or large saucepan containing enough boiling water to come halfway up the sides of the basin. Check the water level periodically and top up with boiling water as necessary.

5 Leave the pudding to stand for 10 minutes before turning out.

SERVES 4–6

TOPPING:
50g muscovado sugar
50g butter, softened

PUDDING:
125g caster or soft brown sugar
125g butter, softened
3 medium free-range eggs
2 tablespoons coffee essence
100g self-raising flour
25g cocoa powder
¼ teaspoon fine sea salt
½ teaspoon baking powder
75g fresh white breadcrumbs

SERVE TOPPED WITH A CONTRASTING WHITE CHOCOLATE SAUCE FOR THE ULTIMATE INDULGENCE

Chocolate sauce

You can make this with dark, milk or white chocolate, provided you use a good quality brand.

1 Break the chocolate into pieces and place in a heatproof bowl (suitable for microwave use) or small saucepan. Pour over the cream.

2 Microwave on High for 1½ minutes or place the saucepan over a very gentle heat until the chocolate has melted. Stir to blend the chocolate with the cream. Cool until tepid. That's it.

100g dark, milk or white chocolate
150ml double cream

Thai rice pudding with coconut and lemon grass

SERVES 4

250g Thai jasmine rice

1 fresh lemon grass stalk, slit almost in half

500ml water

½ teaspoon fine sea salt

100g caster sugar

200ml carton coconut cream

4 tablespoons double cream, plus extra to
serve (optional)

TO SERVE:

mango slices

TOP WITH SLICED FRESH MANGO (AS
ILLUSTRATED), OR SERVE WITH A MANGO
COULIS (PAGE 11) OR CARAMELISED MANGO
SLICES (PAGE 42)

Possibly the fastest rice pudding in the West. I use delicate, fragrant slightly sticky Thai jasmine rice and cook it in salted water in the traditional Thai way, adding sugar and coconut cream afterwards. To enrich it further, I suggest you stir in a little double cream. Serve this pudding warm and creamy, with a tangy mango accompaniment.

1 Put the rice, lemon grass, water and salt into a medium heavy-based saucepan. Bring to the boil, stirring once or twice, then turn the heat to low, cover and simmer for 12 minutes.

2 Remove the pan from the heat and, without removing the lid, leave to stand for 5 minutes.

3 Remove the lemon grass. Add the sugar and stir until dissolved, then stir in the coconut cream. Leave to stand, covered, for a further 5 minutes. Add the double cream.

4 Serve the rice pudding warm rather than hot, adding extra cream if you like. Top with mango slices.

Variation

This is also delicious served cold, as a condé. Leave the rice pudding to cool completely, then stir in some single cream to loosen it. Put a layer of sliced mango, apricots or peaches in the base of 6 sundae dishes and spoon over the rice. Chill lightly before serving, sprinkled with chopped roasted pistachios or almonds.

Peach and cherry trifles

A good trifle should have the texture of a fruit fool – creamy without being at all runny. My favourite trifle has a base of macaroons (or amaretti biscuits) soaked in framboise, layers of sliced fresh peaches and red fruits, and a rich crème anglaise topping that has been whipped to lighten it. For a decadent finish, you can pile floppy whipped cream on top. (Note that this crème anglaise is richer than my standard recipe on page 193.)

1 First, make the crème anglaise. Put the cream and milk in a heavy-based pan with 1 tablespoon of the sugar. Slit the vanilla pod and scrape out the seeds with the tip of a knife, adding them to the pan. Slowly bring to the boil. Meanwhile, beat the remaining sugar and egg yolks together in a large bowl, then gradually pour on a third of the creamy milk, beating constantly.

2 Return this mixture to the pan and cook on a low heat, stirring continuously with a wooden spoon until the custard is thick enough to thinly coat the back of the spoon. Strain the custard into a clean bowl, cover and cool, then chill.

3 Skin the peaches for the trifle: dip in boiling water for 30 seconds then into cold water; remove and slip off the skins. Halve and stone the peaches, then slice thinly.

4 Crush the macaroons or amaretti biscuits and divide between 6 wine glasses. Sprinkle over the framboise or sherry and press the biscuits down lightly. Layer the sliced peaches and red fruit on top. Chill for 30 minutes.

5 Using a balloon whisk or electric whisk, beat the chilled crème anglaise until fluffy, then divide between the wine glasses.

6 Whip the cream with the icing sugar, if using, and spoon on top of each trifle in a lovely languid dollop. Serve lightly chilled.

SERVES 6

CREME ANGLAISE:
300ml double cream
100ml milk
50g caster sugar
1 vanilla pod
6 large free-range egg yolks

TRIFLE:
2 large ripe peaches
100g macaroons or amaretti biscuits
6 tablespoons framboise eau-de-vie, or medium dry sherry
150g pitted cherries, raspberries or other red fruit

TO SERVE (OPTIONAL):
150ml whipping cream
2 teaspoons icing sugar

Golden apple streusel tart

SERVES 6

1 quantity Pâte sucrée (page 202)

4–5 large Granny Smith or Golden Delicious
   apples

50g butter

3–4 tablespoons Calvados

100g sultanas

150g raspberries (optional)

STREUSEL TOPPING:

75g plain flour

$\frac{1}{2}$ teaspoon ground cinnamon

40g butter

40g demerara sugar

2 tablespoons chopped roasted hazelnuts,
   or 2 digestive biscuits, finely crushed

CREME CHANTILLY (PAGE 50) IS THE
PERFECT ACCOMPANIMENT TO THIS
STREUSEL TART

Apple tarts seldom fail to please my guests. This recipe is a cross between a flan and a crumble. As it's quite crumbly, you will find it easier to slice using a hot, large cook's knife – simply dip in a jug of boiling water, then dry and use quickly.

1 Roll out the pâte sucrée thinly and use to line a 21cm flan tin, 3–3.5cm deep, with removable base. Leave the edges untrimmed and overhanging. Line the pastry case with foil and baking beans, then chill for 20 minutes. Preheat the oven to 190°C, Gas 5.

2 Meanwhile, quarter, core and peel the apples, then cut into 2cm dice. Heat the butter in a large frying pan until sizzling. Toss in the apple cubes and sauté for about 5–7 minutes until golden brown and slightly softened. Add the Calvados, stirring to deglaze, and cook until all the liquid has evaporated. Set aside to cool.

3 Stand the flan tin on a baking sheet and bake the pastry case blind for 15 minutes, then remove from the oven and take out the foil and beans. Lower the oven setting to 170°C, Gas 3. With a sharp knife, trim the pastry level with the top of the flan tin. Spoon in the apples and scatter over the sultanas and raspberries, if using.

4 To make the streusel topping, sift the flour with the cinnamon into a bowl. Now rub in the butter until the mixture resembles fine breadcrumbs. Stir in the sugar and nuts or crushed biscuits. Spoon this topping over the fruits in an even layer.

5 Bake the flan for 30 minutes until the topping is crisp and golden. Transfer the flan tin to a wire rack and leave to cool slightly. To unmould, press up the base of the tin and slide the streusel tart on to a large plate. Serve warm, with crème chantilly.

Little treacle tarts

MAKES 24 MINI TARTS
300g golden syrup

85g fresh white breadcrumbs

60g ground almonds

1 large free-range egg, beaten

150ml double cream

½ quantity Pâte sucrée (page 202)

about 4 tablespoons raspberry or apricot jam, slightly warmed

This cross between a bakewell tart and an American pecan pie gives the great British treacle tart a neat update. I add eggs and almonds to the filling to hold it together and bake it in a pâte sucrée base. This was the dessert I served to President Putin when he visited Prime Minister Blair back in the spring of 2000. He must have enjoyed it because he insisted I posed with him for a photo call. Will it become a Kremlin favourite I wonder? You can either make 24 baby tarts in mini muffin tins, or one large tart to serve 6–8.

1 Put the golden syrup, breadcrumbs, ground almonds, egg and cream in a food processor or blender and whizz until smooth. For best results, chill this filling for 24 hours.

2 Divide the pastry in half. Roll out each piece on a lightly floured board to a rectangle, about 3mm thick. Drape each pastry sheet loosely over a 12–hole mini muffin tray, with 4–5cm diameter hollows. Set aside for 15–20 minutes to let the softened pastry fall naturally into the holes, then gently ease it into the bases, using a small ball of dough. Do not trim to fit at this stage.

3 Preheat the oven to 180°C, Gas 4. Spoon or pipe about ½ teaspoon of jam into each muffin tin. Spoon or pipe the filling on top to three-quarters fill the pastry cases. Bake for 10 minutes, then lower the heat to 150°C, Gas 2 and bake for a further 10 minutes.

4 Take out the muffin trays and trim the pastry, using a scone cutter the same diameter as the tarts and a sharp knife. Peel away excess pastry.

5 Return the tarts to the oven for a further 10–15 minutes until golden and risen. Leave in the tins for 5–10 minutes to firm up, then gently ease them out and place on a wire rack to cool completely.

Large treacle tart, to serve 6–8

1 You will need only about 350g pâte sucrée. Make the filling as above and chill for 24 hours. Roll out the pâte sucrée and use to line a loose-based 21cm tart tin, at least 2cm deep, letting the pastry overhang the edge of the tin all round; don't trim. Leave to rest for 20 minutes.

2 Preheat the oven to 180°C, Gas 4. Spread the jam over the base of the pastry case and spoon the filling on top. Stand the flan tin on a baking sheet and bake for 15 minutes. Lower the heat to 150°C, Gas 2 and bake for a further 20 minutes.

3 Remove from the oven and trim the pastry level with the top of the tin. Bake for a further 15–20 minutes. Cool in the tin for at least 30 minutes, then push up the removable base and slide the tart on to a plate.

SUPERB SERVED WITH LEMON GRASS FLAVOURED CREME FRAICHE (PAGE 50)

Espresso coffee crème brûlée

Crème brûlée comes in a variety of flavours. In the restaurant we serve basil, rosemary and lavender infused pots. For this coffee-flavoured cream you need to use a set of ovenproof coffee cups – such as the espresso set in the photograph. Chocolate-coated coffee beans add a chic finishing touch.

SERVES 6
350ml double cream
125ml whole milk (preferably UHT)
50ml double strength espresso coffee
1 tablespoon Kahlua or Tia Maria (optional)
6 large free-range egg yolks
75g caster sugar
TO SERVE:
2 tablespoons demerara sugar, to caramelise
chocolate-coated coffee beans (optional)

1 Preheat the oven to 140°C, Gas 1. Lightly grease 6 ovenproof coffee cups and stand them on a baking tray.

2 Put the cream and milk in a heavy-based saucepan and heat slowly to scalding point, then stir in the espresso coffee and liqueur, if using.

3 Beat the egg yolks in a large heatproof bowl until pale and creamy. Pour the hot steaming coffee cream on to the egg yolks, a third at a time, whisking well. Then whisk in the caster sugar. Strain this liquid through a fine-mesh sieve into a jug.

4 Pour the mixture into the coffee cups, dividing it equally. Bake for about 45 minutes until the custards are very lightly set on top. To test, tilt one of the cups slightly: the custard should come away from the side of the cup and the centre should still be slightly wobbly. Remove from the oven and allow to cool; the mixture will thicken on cooling. Chill until required.

5 When ready to serve, sprinkle a teaspoon of demerara sugar evenly over the surface of each custard and caramelise with a blow-torch. Serve as soon as possible, with a few chocolate coffee beans if you like.

Note: If you do not have a blow-torch, it is possible to caramelise the topping by placing the cups under a very hot grill. However, this is only effective if the grill is very hot, otherwise the set custard underneath can melt. If in doubt about your grill or the capacity of the cups to withstand grilling, omit the topping.

Caramelised pear tatin

SERVES 4

6 Conference pears

about 300g Minute puff pastry (page 209),
    Mascarpone flaky pastry (page 208), or a
    good ready-made puff

100g butter, softened

100g caster sugar

We serve baby tarts in the restaurant, cooking them in small copper saucepans, but you can just as easily make a family-sized tart tatin. You will need a shallow metal pan that is suitable for use in the oven, such as a sauté pan, paella pan, cast-iron gratin dish or a proper tart tatin tin – about 21cm in diameter and no deeper than 6cm. The cut pears are refrigerated a good 12 hours ahead so they dry out a little. It doesn't matter if they discolour because the caramel topping will cover them.

1 Peel the pears as thinly and neatly as possible. Cut into quarters and remove the cores. Place in a single layer on a large plate and refrigerate, uncovered, for at least 12 hours, so they dry out a little. (This helps to prevent the pears giving out too much juice during cooking that might dilute the caramel.)

2 The next day, roll out the pastry on a board to a 24cm round (using a cake tin as a template). Cover with cling film and chill for 1-2 hours.

3 Spread the butter thickly over the base of a 21cm tart tatin tin or other ovenproof pan (see above). Sprinkle over the sugar in an even layer. Press the pear quarters into the butter, cut-side uppermost, arranging them in a circle with one in the centre.

4 Now, place the pan over a medium heat and cook, without stirring, so the butter and sugar melt together to make a caramel syrup. Shake the pan from time to time to encourage the caramel to form. Cook for about 10 minutes until the pears start to soften, then remove from the heat.

5 Preheat the oven to 200°C, Gas 6. Using a rolling pin, lift the pastry round over the fruit in the pan and position centrally. Tuck the pastry edges down the side of the pan, enclosing the fruit. Pierce the pastry in a few places with the tip of a sharp thin-bladed knife.

6 Bake for 15 minutes, then turn the heat down to 180°C, Gas 4 and cook for a further 10–15 minutes until the pastry is golden brown and crisp. (We tip out any excess juices from the pan halfway through cooking to prevent them from diluting the caramel sauce. If you do this, take care to avoid burning your arm with the hot caramel.)

7 Leave the tart to stand for 10 minutes, then invert on to a large flat serving plate. Serve warm.

TART TATIN IS BEST SERVED WARM, WITH SCOOPS OF VANILLA ICE CREAM, WHIPPED CREAM OR CREME FRAICHE

Deep-dish autumn fruit pie

I like to keep the fruits chunky for this top-crust pie, and pan-roast them first with butter and sugar to enhance the flavour. The pastry is my favourite orange flower water recipe. You'll need a 1.2 litre pie dish, about 23cm in diameter. An ideal dessert to round off Sunday lunch.

1 Roll out the pastry to a 5mm thickness, 2–3cm larger all round than your 1.2 litre pie dish. Turn the pie dish upside down on the pastry and cut out a pie lid just slightly bigger than the dish. Slide on to a baking sheet, cover with cling film and set aside. Re-roll the trimmings and cut into long 1cm wide strips; cover and set these aside too.

2 Peel the apples and pears thinly. Quarter and core them, then cut into thick chunks. Halve and stone the peaches or plums, then cut into quarters if you like; there's no need to peel them.

3 Pan-roast the fruit in two batches. Heat 30g butter in a frying pan, add half the fruit and sprinkle with half of the sugar and spice. Sauté gently for about 5 minutes until just softened, then spoon into the pie dish. Repeat with the remaining butter, fruit, sugar and spice.

4 Position a pie funnel, if you have one, in the middle of the fruit (this helps to hold the pastry up so it cooks crisply). Set aside to cool.

5 To finish making the pie, brush the rim of the dish with water and press the pastry strips on to it, pinching the joins together. Brush this pastry rim with the egg glaze. Using a rolling pin, lift the pie lid over the filling, positioning it centrally. If using a pie funnel, nick a small cross in the pastry so it falls evenly over. Press the edges lightly together.

6 Hold the pie dish up in one hand and with a small sharp knife held at an angle away from the dish, cut away the overhanging pastry. Roll your index finger into a knuckle and press down firmly all round the edge. As you do this, knock up the pastry edge by slashing it horizontally all round with a table knife – to look like light leaves of pastry.

7 Traditionally, sweet pies are baked without further adornment, but you can add finishing touches. For a scalloped edge, pinch the pastry edge with your thumb and forefinger, gently pushing it in with the back of a knife. Cut out leaves or other shapes from the rolled-out trimmings too, if you like. Brush the pastry lid with egg glaze, including the edge. Apply any decorations and glaze these too. Sprinkle lightly with sugar and chill for 20 minutes. Meanwhile, preheat the oven to 190°C, Gas 5.

8 Stand the pie on a baking sheet and bake for 35–40 minutes until the crust is crisp and golden brown. Lower the temperature slightly towards the end of cooking if the pastry appears to be browning too quickly. Leave to stand for 20 minutes before serving.

SERVES 6

1 quantity Fragrant orange pastry (page 203)

3 large Granny Smith apples

3 large Conference pears

4 large peaches, or 8 large red plums

60g butter

60g caster sugar

1 teaspoon Chinese five-spice powder

TO GLAZE:

1 free-range egg yolk, beaten with 2 teaspoons water

1–2 teaspoons caster sugar

CREME ANGLAISE (PAGE 193), POURING CREAM OR VANILLA ICE CREAM (PAGE 57) WOULD MAKE THIS A PERFECT PUDDING

special occasions

Orange pannacottas

If you enjoy a light custard, then try Italian pannacotta, which is basically a chic blancmange. It is set with leaf gelatine and is easier to make than either crème caramel or crème brûlée. We serve pannacottas softly set so they have an irresistible sexy wobble as they are carried to the table (we call this chi-chi-lina in the kitchen). I like to accompany them with roasted figs and orange segments, though you may prefer fresh berries.

1 Put the glucose, half of the sugar and the water in a heavy-based saucepan. Dissolve slowly over a low heat, stirring once or twice. Using a pastry brush dipped in warm water, brush down the side of the pan occasionally to dislodge any sugar crystals that might otherwise cause the syrup to crystallise.

2 When every sugar grain has dissolved, bring to the boil and cook, without stirring, to a light golden brown caramel. (On a sugar thermometer, it should register 125°C.) As soon as it reaches this stage, remove from the heat and plunge the base of the pan into a bowl of cold water to stop further cooking. Set aside to cool. The liquid glucose keeps the syrup viscous and gives it a sheen (see note).

3 Place 6 small dariole moulds, about 120ml capacity, on a baking tray.

4 Put the cream and milk in a large saucepan and bring slowly to the boil. Once the liquid starts to creep up the side of the pan, adjust the heat so it maintains a steady boil. Cook for about 5 minutes to reduce by about a third.

5 Meanwhile, soak the gelatine sheets in a bowl of cold water for about 5 minutes until they become floppy. Remove and gently squeeze out excess water.

6 Take the boiling cream off the heat and add the remaining sugar, orange zest and gelatine leaves, stirring until dissolved. Allow to cool, then mix in the liqueur or rum.

7 Spoon the cooled caramel into the base of the dariole moulds, then slowly pour in the creamy milk mixture. Chill until set.

8 When ready to serve, gently pull the side of each pannacotta away from the mould, invert on to a plate and shake to release. A topping of orange zest confit strips is so effective. Serve with honey roasted figs and orange segments, or berry fruits.

Note: We store this syrup in squeezy bottles in the restaurant and trickle it over desserts as we lay them out. The liquid glucose keeps it flowing.

SERVES 6

4 tablespoons liquid glucose
300g caster sugar
3 tablespoons water
600ml double cream
150ml milk
3 sheets of leaf gelatine
grated zest of 2 oranges
2 tablespoons Cointreau or white rum

TO SERVE:

orange zest confit strips (page 47), optional
Honey roasted figs (page 42), optional
fresh orange segments, strawberries or
 raspberries

DELECTABLE WITH HONEY ROASTED FIGS
(PAGE 42), FRESH ORANGE SEGMENTS AND
ORANGE ZEST CONFIT (PAGE 47)

Chocolate mocha tart

SERVES 6–8

1 quantity Chocolate pastry (page 203)

200g dark chocolate (about 60% cocoa solids),
   melted

SPONGE LAYER:

1 large free-range egg white

2 teaspoons powdered egg white

40g caster sugar

50g ground almonds

1 tablespoon plain flour, sifted

2 tablespoons coffee essence

2 tablespoons Tia Maria

MOCHA CUSTARD:

120ml double cream

4 tablespoons milk

2 tablespoons strong fresh coffee, cooled

1 large free-range egg, beaten

50g caster sugar

SUBLIME WITH SOFTLY WHIPPED CREME
CHANTILLY (PAGE 50) AND A FEW
RASPBERRIES OR ORANGE SEGMENTS

There are three parts to this tart: a meltingly smooth chocolate pastry base, a light coffee and liqueur soaked sponge, and a crowning of rich velvety chocolate custard. I don't pretend it's a quick recipe, but the three stages are all quite straightforward. I would advise you to make the tart case and sponge disc well ahead, leaving the topping until a few hours before serving. This is a recipe you will return to, time and again.

1 First, make a template for the sponge layer. Line a baking sheet with baking parchment. Lay the removable base of a 21cm flan tin on the parchment and draw round it. Return the base to the flan tin.

2 Roll out the pastry on a lightly floured surface and use to line the 21cm flan tin, which must be 3–3.5cm deep. As the dough is soft you may find it easier to pat it out after some initial rolling; pinch any cracks together. Don't trim the edge, leave it overhanging. Prick the base, then line with foil and baking beans. Chill for 15–20 minutes.

3 Preheat the oven to 190°C, Gas 5. Stand the flan tin on a baking sheet and bake blind for 15 minutes. Remove the foil and beans, trim the pastry edge level with the top of the tin and bake for a further 10 minutes until crisp. Cool. Turn the oven setting down to 170°C, Gas 3.

4 Spread a third of the melted chocolate evenly over the pastry base. Keep the remaining chocolate runny, at room temperature.

5 Now make the sponge layer. Whisk the egg white and powder in a bowl until softly stiff, then whisk in the sugar until glossy and firm. Using a large metal spoon, carefully fold in the ground almonds and flour. Spread the mixture over the circle on the parchment (or pipe using a large plain nozzle). Bake for 12 minutes. Leave to stand for 5 minutes, then carefully peel off the paper and cool on a wire rack. Heat the coffee essence and liqueur until hot but not boiling, then cool.

6 For the custard, bring the cream and milk to the boil in a pan, then pour on to the remaining melted chocolate, stirring until smooth. Cool, then stir in the coffee. Beat the egg with the sugar, then mix with the chocolate cream.

7 When ready to assemble, heat the oven to 150°C, Gas 2. Fit the sponge disc into the pastry case and spoon over the coffee liqueur syrup. Place the flan tin on its baking sheet on the middle oven shelf, pulling the shelf out as far as it is safe. Pour in the chocolate custard – it should reach the top. Gently push the oven shelf back and bake for about 40 minutes. The filling will be soft – it becomes firmer on cooling.

8 Cool until the filling is the consistency of softly whipped cream. Unmould the tart on to a large flat plate and serve at room temperature.

Pumpkin cheesecake

This is a lightly baked cheesecake, cooked on a thin disc of sponge. It is a very pretty colour and is probably best served simply with a light dusting of icing sugar. However, as pumpkins are autumn food, you might like to serve it with a spoonful or two of roasted pears or plums. For a rich pumpkin flavour, I suggest you prepare the purée ahead and freeze it. On thawing, the pulp separates out and you can discard the watery fluid leaving full-flavoured pumpkin flesh.

1 First, prepare the pumpkin purée for the filling. Remove the seeds and stringy centre from the pumpkin, then peel away the skin as thinly as possible. Cut the flesh into small cubes. Heat the butter in a frying pan, add the pumpkin with 25g of the sugar and cook for about 10 minutes until softened. Transfer to a food processor and work until smooth. Allow to cool. You can make this purée a day or so ahead and freeze it to concentrate the flavour (see above).

2 For the sponge base, preheat the oven to 200°C, Gas 6. Whisk the egg whites in a bowl until softly stiff. Gradually fold in the caster sugar, then the egg yolks. Sift the cornflour and flour together over the mixture and then fold in carefully.

3 Line a baking sheet with baking parchment. Spread the sponge mixture out to an area approximately 30cm square – it needs to be an even thickness, but not necessarily a neat square. Bake for 7–10 minutes until golden brown and springy when pressed. Invert on to a wire rack to cool and then peel off the paper. Lower the oven setting to 170°C, Gas 3.

4 For the cheesecake you will need a 23–24cm springform cake tin, that is about 6cm deep. Cut out a round from the sponge base to fit exactly inside the tin, using the base of the tin as a guide. It is preferable to cut the sponge a little larger and trim it to fit, rather than cut it smaller and leave gaps that the pumpkin filling might leak through.

5 For the filling, beat the mascarpone, crème fraîche, soured cream, 50g of the remaining sugar, the vanilla seeds (or extract) and 2 egg yolks together in a bowl until evenly blended. Stir in the pumpkin purée.

6 Whisk the 2 egg whites in another bowl until softly stiff. Gradually whisk in the remaining 25g sugar and gently fold into the pumpkin mixture. Pour the filling over the sponge base in the tin and bake for 40–50 minutes until lightly firm on top.

7 Leave the cheesecake to cool and then chill in the tin. Run a table knife around the inside of the tin and carefully unmould on to a flat plate. Serve in wedges, dusted lightly with icing sugar.

SERVES 6–8

SPONGE BASE:

3 medium free-range eggs, separated

70g caster sugar

40g cornflour

40g strong plain flour

FILLING:

about 700g fresh unpeeled pumpkin

50g butter

100g caster or light soft brown sugar

200g mascarpone

125ml crème fraîche

70ml soured cream

seeds from 2 vanilla pods, or 1 teaspoon vanilla extract

2 large free-range eggs, separated

TO SERVE:

icing sugar, sifted, to dust

SERVE SIMPLY DUSTED WITH ICING SUGAR, OR WITH ROASTED PLUMS (PAGE 41), SLOW ROASTED PEARS (PAGE 43) OR A QUENELLE OF ORANGE FLOWER WATER ICE CREAM (PAGE 59)

Summer berry filo horns

SERVES 4

2–3 sheets of filo pastry, measuring about
   28 x 40cm
about 100g butter, melted
5 tablespoons icing sugar, sifted, plus extra to
   dust
400g raspberries
400g small ripe strawberries
250g mascarpone
250ml crème fraîche
300ml double cream

TO SERVE:

Strawberry or raspberry coulis (page 11)
soft fruits, such as strawberries, raspberries
   and redcurrants

SERVE WITH STRAWBERRY OR RASPBERRY
COULIS (PAGE 11) AND SUMMER BERRIES

Even the heaviest pastry cook in the kingdom is safe with filo. All you need to be is a dab hand with a butter-dipped pastry brush. Shape buttery filo squares around metal cream horn moulds and bake until crisp, cool and then pipe in a flavoured berry cream – or another flavoured cream, such as Pistachio cream (page 52). Serve one or two per person, with a red fruit coulis and soft summer fruits alongside. Include some flavourful wild strawberries if they are available.

1 Preheat the oven to 190°C, Gas 5. Cut out ten 12cm squares from the pastry. Work with one filo square at a time; keep the others covered with cling film to stop them drying out. Lightly brush one filo square with butter and dust lightly with icing sugar.

2 Wrap the square of filo, buttered side out, around a cream horn mould to form a cornet. Keep the wrapping slightly loose so that the cornet will slide off once it is cooked. Also, don't let the filo extend beyond the rim of the mould. Place on a non-stick baking sheet and repeat with the rest of the filo to shape 10 cornets (this allows for breakages).

3 Bake the filo cornets for about 12–15 minutes until golden brown and crisp. Leave to cool for a few minutes, then carefully slide them off the moulds on to a wire rack and cool completely.

4 Put the raspberries and strawberries in a bowl and crush them with a fork, then add the icing sugar. Beat the mascarpone, crème fraîche and double cream together in another bowl until smooth and then fold in the fruit crush. Spoon into a piping bag fitted with a large plain nozzle and set aside until ready to serve.

5 To serve, simply pipe the berry cream into the filo cornets and dust lightly with icing sugar. Spoon a little strawberry or raspberry coulis on to each dessert plate and arrange the filo cornets on the plates with a pile of soft fruits alongside.

Tiramisu in two ways

SERVES 6

VANILLA CREAM:

100g caster sugar

5 tablespoons water

3 free-range egg yolks

250g mascarpone

100ml crème fraîche

5 tablespoons Greek yogurt

1 vanilla pod

300ml double cream

TO ASSEMBLE:

350g Marinated cherries (page 13)

grated dark chocolate, to sprinkle

OR FOR A TRADITIONAL TIRAMISU:

200ml strong fresh coffee, cooled

3 tablespoons rum

about 12 Italian sponge finger biscuits

50g grated dark chocolate

In the restaurant we sometimes pipe a tiramisu-style cream into little chocolate cases and serve them as petits fours. This cream, however, is very versatile and is particularly good spooned over marinated cherries in dainty wine glasses. You can also layer it with sponge fingers dipped in a coffee rum sauce to make a more traditional tiramisu. If you opt for the latter, do buy the proper Italian savoyardi biscuits as they hold their shape better when dipped and layered.

1 To make the vanilla cream, put the sugar and water in a small heavy-based pan and dissolve over a low heat. Increase the heat and boil for about 5 minutes until the syrup reaches 120°C – the 'hard ball' stage, when a small teaspoonful of syrup dropped into ice-cold water forms a firm, clear ball.

2 Using a hand-held electric mixer, whisk the egg yolks in a heatproof bowl placed on a damp cloth to hold it steady. When the yolks start to become thick and pale, reheat the sugar syrup briefly and trickle down the side of the bowl as you whisk. Continue to whisk for a further 3–4 minutes, then remove and cool.

3 Put the mascarpone, crème fraîche and yogurt in a bowl. Slit the vanilla pod open and scrape out the seeds, adding them to the bowl. Beat well, then gently mix into the cooled egg yolk mixture.

4 Whip the cream in a bowl until softly stiff, then fold into the mixture with a large metal spoon. Cover and chill until ready to serve.

Tiramisu with marinated cherries

Divide the marinated cherries between wine glasses, then simply dollop spoonfuls of the tiramisu cream on top in soft floppy peaks. Sprinkle with a little grated dark chocolate to serve.

Traditional tiramisu

If you intend to go the full Monty, here's how. Mix the coffee and rum in a shallow bowl. Quickly dunk half of the sponge fingers in the liquid, one at a time, and make a single layer in a pretty glass bowl. Spoon over half the tiramisu cream. Dunk the remaining sponge fingers in the same way and arrange on top. Spoon over the remaining cream, then dredge with the chocolate. Chill for at least 2 hours before serving. Wait for the accolades.

Lemon and passion fruit tartlets

'Classic French lemon tarts' that you can buy somehow lack the zing of home-baked ones, so make the effort once in a while when you want to impress. In the case of curd tarts, the filling sets on cooling so don't be alarmed if it's still a little runny when you take them out of the oven. For crisp cases, bake the tartlet cases blind, then pour in the filling and bake on a low setting so the cream remains a paler shade of yellow.

1 Divide the pastry into 6 portions and knead lightly into rounds. Roll out thinly and use to line six 10cm tartlet tins, allowing plenty of overhang. (If the pastry is a little sticky, dip your fingers into icing sugar and pat it out.) Press the dough into the tins, making sure the sides and base are well moulded; if any pastry tears, simply pinch it together. Place the tartlet tins on a baking sheet and chill for 20–30 minutes. Preheat the oven to 180°C, Gas 4.

2 Meanwhile, grate the zest from 2 lemons and reserve; squeeze the juice from all 4 lemons. Scoop the passion fruit pulp into a small pan and add the lemon juice. Bring to the boil and boil to reduce by about a third to 150ml. Pass through a sieve into a bowl, rubbing to extract the juice from the passion fruit seeds. Set aside to cool.

3 Line the tartlet cases with foil and fill with baking beans. Bake the pastry cases blind for 15 minutes. Remove the foil and beans, then trim the pastry edges neatly. Bake for a further 5 minutes, then remove and set aside. Reduce the oven setting to 140°C, Gas 1.

4 Meanwhile, beat the caster sugar, egg yolks and grated lemon zest together in a bowl until pale and creamy, then beat in the cream and trickle in the cooled fruit juice. Don't worry if the mixture curdles a little, it will be fine.

5 Pour the lemon cream into the tartlet cases and bake until the filling looks lightly set, about 30 minutes at this very low heat. Turn off the oven but leave the tarts inside to cool slowly for a good hour. Remove from the oven, leave to cool completely and then chill.

6 For a crisp coating, sift half the icing sugar over the filling and caramelise lightly, using a blow-torch. Sift another layer of icing sugar on top and caramelise in the same way. This finish isn't essential, but it does help to establish your reputation as a culinary genius.

SERVES 6

½ **quantity Pâte sucrée (page 202)**

4 **lemons**

4 **ripe passion fruit, halved**

180g **caster sugar**

6 **free-range egg yolks, beaten**

150ml **double cream**

2 **tablespoons icing sugar, to finish**

CARAMELISED ICING SUGAR GIVES A PROFESSIONAL FINISHING TOUCH

Coffee profiteroles topped with chocolate

SERVES 6

1 quantity Choux pastry (page 205)

FILLING:

½ quantity Crème pâtissière (page 195)

150g dark chocolate, in pieces

3 tablespoons water

4 tablespoons double cream

2 tablespoons coffee essence

3 tablespoons Baileys, Tia Maria or Kahlua (optional)

Choux pastry is deceptively easy. Provided you can weigh, beat and pipe, you will find this dessert a cinch. Make the buns and filling ahead and put them together at the last minute. The filling is simply crème pâtissière with added cream and coffee essence, whisked until light and creamy. For a glossy finish, we dip the buns in melted dark chocolate and serve them before the chocolate sets. They look so tempting.

1 Preheat the oven to 200°C, Gas 6. Line a large, heavy baking sheet with baking parchment. Put the choux pastry into a large piping bag fitted with a large plain nozzle, about 1.5cm. First, pipe a blob of choux paste under each corner of the parchment to hold it in position.

2 Pipe about 20 choux balls, each the size of a walnut, on to the baking sheet spacing them slightly apart to allow for expansion.

3 To level the peaked tops, simply dab the points with a wet finger. Bake the choux balls until well risen and evenly golden brown, about 20 minutes. Transfer to a wire rack to cool completely. (You can make the choux buns well ahead and keep them in an airtight tin, or freeze.)

4 Make the crème pâtissière and cool. When ready to fill the buns, put the chocolate and water in a small heatproof bowl. Microwave on High for about 2 minutes or place over a pan of simmering water to melt the chocolate. Stir until smooth and cool until tepid.

5 Using a hand-held mixer, beat the cream and coffee essence into the cooled crème pâtissière until smooth and creamy, then incorporate the liqueur if using. Spoon into a piping bag, fitted with a small plain nozzle. Use the tip of the nozzle to pierce a hole in the base of each choux bun and pipe in the filling.

6 Just before serving, dip the top of each bun into the melted chocolate to coat. Place on a large serving plate or individual dessert plates.

Vacherins of strawberries with a passion fruit cream

A vacherin is a shallow basket of meringue filled with a flavoured whipped cream and fresh fruits such as wild strawberries or other berries. The bases can easily be made a day or two ahead and kept in an airtight tin. We like to bake these in a very low oven so the meringue merely dries out and remains brilliant white. Our ovens have pilot lights that maintain a really low heat, but modern domestic ovens aren't so lucky. If you happen to have a four-oven Aga, the lowest warming oven should do the honours. Otherwise turn your oven to a 'keep warm' setting and prop the door open slightly with a wooden spoon. If your vacherins bake pale cream before they crisp, don't despair – they will still taste fabulous.

SERVES 6

3 large free-range egg whites (ideally about 1 week old)
small squeeze of lemon juice
150g caster sugar
PASSION FRUIT CREAM:
6 passion fruit
200g mascarpone
150ml crème fraîche
70ml soured cream
a little icing sugar, to sweeten (optional)
150ml double cream
TO SERVE:
about 250g mixed raspberries, redcurrants and sliced wild strawberries (or other small ones)
icing sugar, to dust

1 Turn the oven to its lowest setting, 110°C, Gas ¼ maximum. Line two baking sheets with baking parchment or a silicone cooking liner. Draw 6 circles, 8cm in diameter, on the paper.

2 Whisk the egg whites with the lemon juice in a large clean bowl until they form firm peaks; do not over-whisk or they will become dry and grainy. Gradually whisk in the sugar, a tablespoonful at a time, to make a smooth, glossy meringue.

3 Spoon the meringue into a piping bag fitted with a 1–1.5cm plain nozzle. Pipe in concentric rounds to fill each drawn circle. Pipe 2 rings on the edge of each meringue disc to form baskets.

4 Bake for at least 2 hours, or up to 8 hours if you are using the heat of a pilot light. The exact time will depend on the temperature, but it is easy to tell when the baskets are cooked. Lift one with a palette knife: if it comes away cleanly, feels crisp on the outside and slightly soft inside, the baskets are ready. Leave on the baking sheet for 10 minutes, then carefully peel the meringue baskets off the paper and transfer to a wire rack to cool completely.

5 Meanwhile, make the passion fruit cream. Halve the passion fruit, scoop out the pulp and seeds into a small pan and boil to reduce by half and concentrate the flavour. Tip into a sieve over a bowl and rub with a wooden spoon to extract as much juice as possible; discard the seeds.

6 Beat the mascarpone with the crème fraîche and soured cream. Mix in the passion fruit juice and sweeten with a little icing sugar, if required. Whip the double cream until it is softly stiff and then fold into the passion fruit cream.

7 When ready to serve, spoon the passion fruit cream into the meringue baskets and top with the fruits. A light dusting of icing sugar adds a magical touch.

Almond and cherry Pithiviers

MAKES 2; EACH SERVES 2–3

¹/₃ quantity All-butter puff pastry (page 206),
   or 340g ready-made puff pastry

1 egg yolk, beaten with a good pinch of salt and
   a splash of cold water, to glaze

FILLING:

100g butter, softened

125g icing sugar, sifted

1 large free-range egg

1 free-range egg yolk

125g ground almonds

15g cornflour

2 tablespoons kirsch

about 100g Marinated cherries (page 13),
   or morello cherries in syrup, well drained

Pithiviers is a town near Orleans famous for this almond pâtisserie. It is based on the tradition of serving a Gâteau de Roi (made in the shape of a crown) in the New Year complete with a little token nestling inside the frangipane. The winner of the token becomes king or queen for the night. Thierry, my pastry chef, tells me you should cut the cake covered with a napkin so no one can cheat and spot the token beforehand.

Pithiviers calls for my all-butter puff pastry that holds a definite shape. Marinated fresh cherries are ideal for the filling. Alternatively, you could buy a jar of Morello cherries in syrup; drain well and spike with kirsch.

1 To make the filling, cream the butter and icing sugar together in a bowl until pale and light, then beat in the egg and egg yolk. Mix the ground almonds with the cornflour and stir into the mixture with the kirsch.

2 Pat the cherries dry with kitchen paper, then mix into the cream filling. Divide in half and shape each piece into a ball. Chill or freeze until firm.

3 Divide the puff pastry in half; re-wrap one half and set aside. Cut the other portion roughly in half, so one piece is slightly larger. Roll out the bigger piece until it is large enough to cut out a 13cm round. Using a removable flan base as a guide, cut out the 13cm pastry round neatly.

4 Roll out the slightly smaller piece a little more thinly and cut out a second round, about 11cm in diameter.

5 Place the smaller pastry round on a baking tray lined with baking parchment. Put a ball of filling in the centre and brush the surrounding pastry with egg glaze. Massage the outer part of the larger pastry round to make it more pliable.

6 Position this round over the filling so the pastry edges meet. Mould it gently around the filling so there are no air pockets and press the edges firmly to seal. You should have a rim about 4cm wide.

7 Cut a scalloped pastry edge with the back of a round-bladed knife, then score radiating lines around the rim. Now, score a pattern of curved lines radiating from the centre – do not cut through the pastry, just mark it. When you look down on the gâteau it should resemble the crown of one of the three kings of the Orient, or the turban of a Middle Eastern vizier. Repeat with the remaining pastry and filling to make a second pie. Chill for a good 30 minutes whilst you preheat the oven to 220°C, Gas 7.

8 Brush the Pithiviers evenly with the remaining egg glaze. Bake for 15 minutes until golden brown, then lower the oven setting to 190°C, Gas 5 and bake for a further 10–15 minutes. Leave on the baking sheet for 10 minutes then carefully slide onto a wire rack to cool completely. Cut each Pithiviers into 2 or 3 portions to serve.

Summer pudding stacks

British summer pudding may be one of the best desserts ever, but I still can't quite bring myself to make it with floppy white bread. Instead, I dip small rounds of thinly sliced brioche in blackcurrant coulis and layer them with a selection of soft fruits in season. Served freshly made – with more fruits and trickles of the coulis – it is just as delicious but lighter than a traditional British summer pud and easier to serve. You will need a deep plain round cutter about 5–6cm in diameter.

1 Cut off all the crusts from the brioche loaf, then cut the loaf into 8 long thin slices. (If you chill the loaf overnight you will find it easier to slice.) Pour the blackcurrant coulis into a shallow dish.

2 Using a 5–6cm cutter, cut out 24 rounds from the brioche (three from each slice).

3 Prepare the fruits to layer in between. Slice the strawberries crossways into rounds; halve blackberries and blueberries. (This enables them to lie flat between the brioche layers.) Sprinkle lightly with sugar if the fruits are tart.

4 Lay a small square of baking parchment (about 8cm) on a board, then place the cutter on top. Briefly dip a brioche round into the blackcurrant coulis to coat all over, then place in the base of the cutter.

5 Arrange a layer of overlapping strawberry slices in the cutter and cover with another coulis-dipped brioche round. Make a layer of blackberries and blueberries on top, and repeat the coulis-dipped brioche layer. Don't make the layers too wet or the stack won't hold up on the plate. You should have 3 layers of brioche and 2 fruit layers. Press down lightly to firm.

6 Using a palette knife, slide the stack on to a serving plate and carefully remove the cutter and paper. Repeat to make the other stacks. Top with raspberries and trickles of coulis to serve.

SERVES 8

1 large homemade Brioche loaf (page 210), or 400g ready-made brioche

2 x quantity Blackcurrant coulis (page 12)

250g strawberries (preferably medium-large), hulled

75g blackberries or redcurrants, stripped of stalks

75g blueberries

a little caster sugar (optional)

TO SERVE:

125g small raspberries

Dark and delicious chocolate torte

SERVES 6–8

TO COAT THE TIN:

25g butter, melted

25g dark chocolate, grated

TORTE:

350g dark chocolate (about 60% cocoa solids)

1 tablespoon instant coffee

2 tablespoons boiling water

2–3 tablespoons brandy

4 large free-range eggs, separated

100g unsalted butter, softened

good pinch of salt

200g caster sugar

SERVE WITH POURING CREAM OR THIN
HALF-FAT CREME FRAICHE

It seems every chef must have his or her ultimate orgiastic chocolate recipe with names like chocolate decadence, indulgence or nemesis. Well, this is mine. It is based on the little hot chocolate fondants we serve in the winter and it occurred to me that if I dropped the flour and cocoa and baked it as a whole torte to be eaten cool it might just become a dinner party favourite. You will find that the top bakes to a slight crispness, which when turned out becomes a light crunchy base.

1 To prepare the cake tin, cut a disc of baking parchment to fit the base of a 20cm round springform cake tin or a moule à manqué tin; set the paper aside. Brush the inside of the tin with the melted butter and chill until set. Coat the side with the grated chocolate, tapping out any excess. Fit the disc of baking parchment on the base. Set aside.

2 For the torte, break up the chocolate and place in a large heatproof bowl. Dissolve the coffee in the boiling water, then stir in the brandy and pour over the chocolate. Microwave for about 2 minutes on High or stand the bowl over a pan of gently simmering water until the chocolate has melted. Stir until smooth and set aside to cool. Preheat the oven to 180°C, Gas 4.

3 Beat the egg yolks and butter together in a bowl until creamy, then beat in the cooled chocolate mixture.

4 In another bowl, whisk the egg whites with the pinch of salt until softly stiff, then gradually whisk in the sugar until you have a firm, glossy meringue.

5 Carefully fold this meringue into the chocolate mixture, about a third at a time, until it is evenly incorporated. Spoon the mixture into the prepared cake tin and gently level the surface. Bake for approximately 40 minutes until risen and the top is crispy. The torte might crack a little, which is fine, and the mixture underneath will still be soft. That is as it should be.

6 Now, turn off the oven and leave the cake to cool slowly inside for about an hour. Remove and cool completely, but do not chill – this torte should be moist and soft.

7 To unmould, run a table knife around the side of the torte to loosen it, then invert on to a serving plate. Cut into wedges, with a knife dipped into hot water.

Strawberry tart with balsamic vinegar

I recognise that when you are entertaining there are no useful commis chefs at your disposal. The chic individual puddings we serve in the restaurant are hardly practical when you are entertaining. So, like most of the recipes in this chapter, this tart is prepared and served whole – simply take it to the table and divide it up there. You can use either my orange flower water pastry or pâte sucrée for the base. The former gives a more shortbread base; the latter is lighter and crisper. After baking, the tart case is filled with a smooth fresh strawberry mousse and topped with fresh strawberries tossed in aged balsamic vinegar. Note that this recipe contains lightly cooked eggs.

SERVES 4–6

1 quantity Fragrant orange pastry (page 203),
    or Pâte sucrée (page 202)
400g strawberries, hulled
3 sheets of leaf gelatine
2 large free-range eggs, beaten
3 free-range egg yolks
80g caster sugar
75g butter, softened
2 tablespoons aged balsamic vinegar

1 Roll out the pastry to a 3mm thickness and use to line a 20cm flan tin, 3–3.5cm deep, with removable base. Leave the edges untrimmed and overhanging. Prick the base lightly with a fork, then line with foil and baking beans. Chill for 20 minutes. Preheat the oven to 190°C, Gas 5.
2 Stand the flan tin on a baking sheet and bake the pastry case blind for 15 minutes, then remove the foil and beans. Using a sharp knife, trim the pastry edge level with the top of the tin. Return to the oven for 10 minutes or until the pastry is cooked. Leave to cool.
3 For the filling, set aside half of the strawberries – reserving the best looking fruit. Purée the rest in a food processor or blender and pass through a sieve if you prefer to remove the seeds.
4 Soak the gelatine sheets in a bowl of cold water for 5 minutes until they become floppy.
5 Meanwhile, heat the strawberry purée in a saucepan until almost boiling. Beat the eggs, egg yolks and sugar together in a bowl until creamy. Pour on the strawberry purée, beating well, then return to the pan and stir over a very low heat for about 3 minutes until thickened slightly. Remove from the heat.
6 Take the gelatine leaves from the bowl and squeeze gently to remove excess water. Slip them into the hot strawberry mixture, whisking until dissolved. Pass through a sieve into a bowl and set aside to cool to room temperature.
7 Beat the butter until it is very soft, then gradually work in the cooled strawberry mixture. Pour into the flan case and chill to set.
8 Meanwhile, slice the reserved strawberries and toss with the balsamic vinegar. When ready to serve, carefully push up the base of the tin and slide the tart on to a serving plate. Arrange the strawberry slices on top.

Chilled summer berries with sabayon gratin

SERVES 6

500–600g assorted summer berries, such as strawberries, raspberries, blackberries, redcurrants and blueberries

2–3 tablespoons crème de pêche (optional)

SABAYON:

6 large free-range egg yolks

90g icing sugar, sifted

1 tablespoon tepid Champagne or water

$\frac{1}{2}$ teaspoon cornflour

1 tablespoon liquid glucose

For a light summer dessert, scatter a mixture of small summer berries over dessert plates and spoon over soft floats of sabayon sauce. A splash of Champagne makes it extra special – engage that last glass of fizz you can't manage after a party. For convenience, you can make the sabayon in advance and chill it. To maximise the effect, make sure the berries are chilled, whip the sabayon until fluffy before spooning it over the fruit, then caramelise to an inviting golden brown. A blow-torch is perfect for this – many kitchen equipment suppliers now sell these.

1 Pick over the berries, hull them if necessary and chill in the refrigerator while you prepare the sabayon.

2 To make the sabayon, place all the ingredients in a large heatproof bowl over a pan of gently simmering water. Using a balloon whisk or small hand-held electric whisk, slowly and steadily whisk the mixture until it starts to turn a pale cream colour.

3 Increase your speed and continue whisking to a pale stable foam. As you lift the beaters, they should trail a ribbon of foam that's almost possible to write with. This will take about 10 minutes.

4 Remove the bowl from the heat and cool, whisking occasionally until tepid. Once the sabayon is cold, cover and chill. (It will hold for a good day in the fridge.)

5 Just before serving, toss the berries with the crème de pêche, if using. Scatter the berries over 6 dessert plates.

6 Whisk the sabayon until thick and fluffy, then spoon over the berries. If you have a blow-torch, wave it quickly over the surface to brown the sabayon. Serve immediately.

Variation

Replace the berries with 125g redcurrants and 3–4 ripe peaches. Make the sabayon as above. Strip the redcurrants from their stalks and poach in 3–4 tablespoons Stock syrup (page 200) for a few minutes until they start to burst. Slice the peaches thinly, place on dessert plates and drizzle with the redcurrant compote. Whisk the sabayon, spoon over the fruit and finish as above.

accompaniments
and chocolates

Nut tuiles

MAKES ABOUT 24

250g ground almonds or hazelnuts

4 large free-range egg whites

50g caster sugar

25g plain flour

Dainty nibbles on the side, such as these tuiles, transform a simple fruit dessert, mousse or ice cream into something superb. According to how you intend to serve them, shape 'mill pond' flat tuiles, lightly curled tuiles or baskets. The latter are perfect for serving ice creams or sorbets.

1 Sift the ground nuts through a fine sieve. Preheat the oven to 180°C, Gas 4. Place a silicone cooking liner (silplat or bake-o-glide) on a large baking sheet. Or you can line the baking sheet with baking parchment, though I find this isn't quite as effective.

2 Whisk the egg whites in a bowl until frothy (but not to a foam). Beat in the sugar, flour and ground nuts until smooth. You will need to shape and bake the tuiles in batches.

3 Using a warmed, shallow dessertspoon, take a teaspoonful of mixture and place on the prepared baking sheet. Spread into a neat round, using the back of the warm spoon. Repeat to shape no more than 5 or 6 rounds, leaving space in between to allow for spreading.

4 Bake for about 7 minutes until golden brown around the edges. Leave on the baking sheet for a few seconds before lifting off with a spatula. Shape the tuiles as required (see below) and allow to cool. They will become crisp on cooling. Repeat to use up the remaining mixture. Tuiles can be stored in an airtight tin for 2–3 days.

Shaping tuiles

FLAT TUILES Place the tuiles on a wire tray and lay a heavy baking sheet on top to keep them flat as they cool.

TUILE BASKETS Shape tuiles in individual brioche tins or other fluted moulds, using another tin to press each tuile into the flutes of the mould (illustrated top right). Carefully unmould once set. Alternatively, you can simply lay each tuile over a small orange and mould gently to form fluted basket shapes.

CURLED TUILES Curve the tuiles around a thin rolling pin, hold in position until set, then carefully lift off and transfer to a wire rack (illustrated bottom left and right).

Variations

Add 1 tablespoon of desiccated coconut, sesame seeds or poppy seeds to the basic mixture before baking.

Hazelnut shortbreads

MAKES ABOUT 20

200g plain flour

¼ teaspoon sea salt

125g unsalted butter, softened

90g caster sugar, plus extra to sprinkle
  (optional)

1 large free-range egg, beaten

50g finely ground roasted hazelnuts

As a Scot, I am naturally partial to good shortbread. In fact, we make shortbreads with a pâte sablé dough or the richer pâte brêton (below). Keep the dough in the fridge (for up to 1 week) and slice off rounds to bake whenever you need fresh biscuits.

1 Sift the flour with the salt. Cream the butter and sugar together using an electric mixer until smooth and creamy. Gradually work in the egg.
2 With the mixer on its slowest setting, add the flour a spoonful at a time, then the nuts. Stop mixing as soon as the dough comes together.
3 Lift the dough on to a sheet of cling film. Shape into a roll, about 4cm in diameter and wrap well. Chill for at least 2 hours until firm.
4 To bake, preheat the oven to 160°C, Gas 3. Slice off rounds of dough, 5mm thick. Place on a non-stick baking sheet and prick lightly with a fork. Bake for about 20 minutes until very pale golden.
5 Leave on the baking sheet for a minute, then lift on to a wire rack. For a classic appearance, sprinkle with sugar as they cool.

Hazelnut and chocolate shortbreads
Dip the cooled shortbreads into 100g melted dark chocolate to half-coat, drain off excess, then leave on baking parchment to set.

Cumin shortbreads

MAKES ABOUT 20

2 large free-range egg yolks

60g caster sugar, plus extra to sprinkle
  (optional)

60g unsalted butter, softened

85g strong plain bread flour

¾ teaspoon baking powder

¾ teaspoon cumin seeds, lightly toasted

These have an amazing melt-in-the-mouth bite and an intriguing flavour. As the pâte brêton dough is quite soft, it is easiest to pat it into shape.

1 Beat the egg yolks and sugar together in a large bowl until thick and creamy. Gradually beat in the butter.
2 Sift the flour and baking powder together into the bowl, scatter in the cumin seeds and mix together. Knead lightly until smooth. Wrap in cling film and chill thoroughly. Preheat the oven to 150°C, Gas 2.
3 On a lightly floured board, roll (or pat) out the dough to a 3mm thickness. To keep the dough cool, I dip my fingers in ice-cold water as I pat it out. Using a 5–6cm cutter, cut out as many rounds as possible. Place these on a non-stick baking sheet and chill for 20 minutes.
4 Prick lightly and sprinkle with a little sugar to glaze, if liked. Bake for 12–15 minutes until golden at the edges. Leave on the baking sheet for a minute, then slide on to a wire rack to cool. Best eaten within 2 days.

Langues de chat

These have some semblance to old-fashioned crisp Barmouth biscuits, except that they are baked as long thin fingers (hence the name 'cat tongues'... sorry). They are wonderful with ice creams and mousses.

MAKES ABOUT 30
60g butter
100g caster sugar
2 large free-range egg whites, lightly beaten
½ teaspoon vanilla extract
70g plain flour

1 Preheat the oven to 160°C, Gas 3. Line a baking sheet with non-stick baking parchment or a silicone cooking liner.
2 Cream the butter and sugar together in a bowl until pale and fluffy. Gradually work in the egg whites, then the vanilla. Mix in the flour until just incorporated – don't over-work the mixture.
3 Spoon the mixture into a piping bag fitted with a 1–1.5cm plain nozzle. Pipe 4–5cm lengths on to the lined baking sheet, spacing them apart to allow for spreading during baking.
4 Bake for 10–12 minutes until golden brown at the edges but still pale golden in the middle. Leave on the baking sheet for a minute or so to firm up slightly, then lift on to a wire rack to cool and crisp. These biscuits can be stored in an airtight container for a few days.

Financiers

These dainty French-style fairy cakes are ideal to accompany desserts. Made with a nut-brown butter for extra flavour, they are baked in little muffin tins. We brush financiers with a caramel syrup, but this isn't essential – a light dusting of icing sugar will do.

MAKES 18–24
125g lightly salted butter
175g caster sugar
125g finely ground almonds
25g plain flour, sifted
50g currants (optional)
3 medium free-range egg whites, lightly beaten

1 Melt the butter in a heavy-based saucepan on a low heat, then raise the heat and cook until the butter is a mid-brown colour. Immediately take off the heat and leave to stand for a few minutes, then carefully pour off the fat into a bowl, leaving the milky solids behind – discard these. Cool the fat to room temperature – it should still be runny.
2 Mix the sugar, ground almonds and flour together in a bowl and stir in the currants if using. Beat in the melted and cooled butter and the egg whites. Cover the bowl and rest the mixture in the fridge for 24 hours.
3 Preheat the oven to 200°C, Gas 6. Lightly grease and flour two 12-hole mini muffin tins. Ladle in the mixture to three-quarters fill the tins. Bake for 8–10 minutes until the cakes are peaked and golden.
4 Cool slightly in the tins, then turn out on to a wire rack whilst still warm. Financiers are best served freshly baked, but they can be stored in an airtight tin for 2–3 days.

Lady's fingers

MAKES ABOUT 20

3 large free-range eggs, separated
70g caster sugar
40g strong plain flour
40g cornflour
icing sugar, to dust

These are simply sponge fingers made from a light whisked sponge. Needless to say they are far superior to their shop-bought counterparts. Serve them with ice creams, or use to make a classic trifle.

1 Preheat the oven to 200°C, Gas 6. Line a large baking sheet with silicone cooking liner or baking parchment.
2 Whisk the egg whites in a bowl to a firm foam, then gradually whisk in the sugar a spoonful at a time. Beat the egg yolks in another bowl and then fold into the meringue.
3 Finally, sift in the flour and cornflour. Carefully fold in, whipping the mixture lightly at the same time to ensure a velvety smooth texture.
4 Spoon into a piping bag fitted with a 1.5cm plain nozzle. Pipe a blob of mixture under each corner of the lining paper to hold it in place on the baking sheet. Then pipe 5–6cm lengths, with space in between.
5 For a pearly finish, sift icing sugar over the sponge fingers and leave to stand for 10 minutes. Bake for 7–10 minutes until pale golden, then dust with icing sugar again.
6 Leave on the baking sheet for a few minutes to firm up, then slide the sponge fingers off on to a wire rack to cool and crisp.

Chocolate lady's fingers
Reduce the quantity of cornflour to 30g, and sift 10g cocoa powder together with the flours.

To use a piping bag: Fit a large plastic piping bag with a nozzle (the right size for the task). Hold the bag in one hand and fold the top down over your hand by a third. Spoon in the mixture to half-fill the bag, pull the empty half up and gently twist the top. As you do so, press the mixture down into the nozzle, making sure it doesn't start to ooze out.

To pipe, hold the bag at an angle with the twisted end between your thumb and forefinger – this is the hand you squeeze with. Hold the nozzle end in your other hand but only gently, to guide it. Keep the nozzle a cm or two above the surface to let the mixture flow out smoothly.

Vanilla macaroons

MAKES ABOUT 60 TINY ONES

140g finely ground almonds

240g icing sugar, sifted

seeds from 2 vanilla pods, or 1 teaspoon vanilla
  extract

2 large egg whites (ideally from 1-week old
  eggs)

1 tablespoon powdered egg white

FILLING (OPTIONAL):

100g mascarpone

100g Greek yogurt

1 tablespoon icing sugar, sifted

100ml double cream

We make hundreds of tiny macaroons each week to serve as petits fours, flavouring them with special chocolate, lemon, strawberry and pistachio flavoured baker's pastes brought over from France. But you can make equally delicious ones with vanilla, or try the chocolate variation. Powdered egg white gives extra strength to the mix – it is available from supermarkets under the name of 'easy egg white'.

1 Line 2 large baking sheets with baking parchment or silicone cooking liners.

2 Mix the ground almonds, icing sugar and vanilla seeds or extract together in a bowl.

3 In another bowl, whisk the egg whites with the powdered egg to a firm foam, then fold in the almond mixture using a large metal spoon. Firmly tap the bowl on the surface to knock out any air pockets.

4 Spoon the mixture into a large piping bag fitted with a 1cm plain nozzle and pipe neat little mounds – around 3cm in diameter would be cute – on to the prepared baking sheets. Press the tops down lightly with a wet spoon if they peak too much. Leave to stand for a good 20 minutes until a skin forms on the surface of each one.

5 Meanwhile, preheat the oven to 150°C, Gas 2. Bake the macaroons on the middle shelf for about 20–25 minutes until they feel slightly firm. Leave on the baking sheets for 5 minutes, then slide off on to a wire tray to cool completely. They shouldn't be crisp all the way through, just nicely chewy. Store in an airtight container for up to 3 days.

6 If you want to sandwich the macaroons together, prepare the filling. Simply beat the mascarpone, yogurt and icing sugar together in a bowl. Whip the cream in another bowl until softly stiff and fold into the mascarpone mixture. Sandwich the macaroons together in pairs with small dabs of this filling just before serving.

Chocolate macaroons

1 Sift 15g plain flour, 25g cocoa powder and 90g icing sugar together into a bowl and stir in 100g ground almonds. In another bowl, whisk 2 large egg whites with 1 tablespoon powdered egg to a firm foam, then whisk in 90g caster sugar a spoonful at a time. Fold in the dry mixture.

2 Shape, bake and cool the macaroons as above.

3 If liked, make a ganache filling. Heat 150ml double cream until almost boiling, then pour on to 150g dark chocolate (in pieces) in a bowl. Stir until melted and smooth, then add 1 tablespoon brandy or rum. Leave until cool and thickened. Sandwich the macaroons together (as above).

Lemon and almond madeleines

MAKES ABOUT 20

75g unsalted butter, softened

3 medium free-range eggs

80g caster sugar

40g ground almonds

80g plain flour

grated zest of 1 lemon

icing sugar, sifted, to dust

Originating from the French region of Lorraine, these light lemon-flavoured cakes are traditionally made with browned butter and baked in shell-shaped moulds. There are numerous variations. My version includes ground almonds, which lend flavour and a deliciously moist texture. Bake them in trays of shell-shaped Madeleine moulds if you have some, or small tartlet or bun tins.

1 Heat the butter slowly in a pan to melt, then raise the heat and cook until it turns a nice golden brown – don't let it burn. Immediately remove from the heat. Leave to stand for 5 minutes, then carefully pour off the fat into a bowl leaving the grainy solids behind; discard these. Cool the fat to room temperature.

2 Using an electric beater, whisk the eggs and sugar together in a bowl until the mixture is pale and thick enough to leave a ribbon trail when the beaters are lifted. This will take 5 minutes or so.

3 Combine the ground almonds, flour and lemon zest in another bowl. Gradually fold in the whisked egg mixture until evenly incorporated. Slowly slip the cooled butter down the side of the bowl and fold in very gently and carefully. Cover and leave the mixture to rest for 2 hours.

4 Meanwhile, preheat the oven to 190°C, Gas 5. Lightly grease and flour two 12-hole Madeleine or bun tin trays. Spoon the mixture into the prepared tins. (If you only have one Madeleine tray, bake the cakes in batches.)

5 Bake for 8–9 minutes until the tops are just firm and springy to the touch. Leave in the tins for 2 minutes, then tip out on to a wire rack to cool. Dust lightly with icing sugar to serve. Madeleines are best served freshly baked but can be stored in an airtight tin for a few days.

Variations

CHOCOLATE Reduce the quantity of flour to 60g and sift together with 20g cocoa powder.

ORANGE Use the grated zest of an orange rather than a lemon.

SERVE CREAMY DESSERTS SUCH AS ICES AND MOUSSES WITH CONTRASTING MADELEINES, NUT TUILES (PAGE 170), LANGUES DE CHAT (PAGE 173), FINANCIERS (PAGE 173) OR SHORTBREADS (PAGE 172) – ALL ILLUSTRATED OVERLEAF

Baby meringues

Here I use a quick French meringue, but you can, of course, opt for the more stable Italian meringue (page 197). In either case you will get a better result if you beat the egg whites with an electric machine rather than a hand-held whisk. The meringues are dried out in a very low oven – timings depend on how low your oven can go. Ideally they should still be white after baking, although I recognise this isn't always possible.

MAKES 24–30
3 large free-range egg whites
small squeeze of lemon juice
150g vanilla sugar (page 129), or plain caster sugar
　　plus 1 teaspoon vanilla extract

1 Turn the oven on to its lowest setting – probably indicated as slow or warm on your oven dial and certainly below 120°C. Line 2 large baking sheets with a silicone cooking liner (such as silpat or bake-o-glide) or baking parchment.

2 Whisk the egg whites with the lemon juice in a very clean large bowl to a glossy foam that holds soft peaks when you lift the beaters up. The foam should be silky, not dry or grainy.

3 Gradually whisk in the sugar, a tablespoonful at a time until it is all incorporated. If using vanilla extract, add it with the last of the sugar. You should have a firm, glossy meringue.

4 Spoon into a large piping bag fitted with a 1.5 cm fluted nozzle. Pipe small stars or whirls, 5–6cm in diameter, on to the prepared baking sheets, spacing them slightly apart to allow for a little expansion. You should be able to pipe 24–30 from this quantity.

5 Bake for about 1½–2 hours, depending on the oven temperature. If the meringues appear to be colouring, then prop the oven door ajar with a wooden spoon handle to lower the temperature inside. Try to keep them as white as you can. The meringues are ready when you can lift one off the liner cleanly. Transfer to wire racks to cool. You will find that they become crisp on the outside as they cool. Serve soon after cooling, or store in an airtight container for up to 5 days.

CHOCOLATES

What is a Dessert book without a section devoted to chocolate? These are possibly the most popular and well used pages in any cookbook. We feature many chocolate desserts in the restaurant and each table receives a small plate of exquisite handmade chocolates with their coffee. These have silky smooth fillings, subtly flavoured with thyme, honey, sesame seeds and even sea salt.

Successful chocolate cooking requires some understanding of the different qualities of chocolate. The quality of a particular chocolate is determined by the variety of cocoa bean and the percentages of cocoa solids or mass (the flavouring element) and cocoa butter (the fat). The percentage of cocoa solids can vary from 30% right up to 80%. The higher the proportion of cocoa solids, the crisper the texture and cleaner the flavour. Chocolate with 70% cocoa solids actually snaps when it is broken. Chocolate with a lower percentage of these solids will have a higher percentage of cocoa butter and other fats and creams. Chocolate with a high proportion of cocoa butter represents the popular end of the confectionery market – the milk chocolates and candies. But don't denigrate milk chocolate. Good quality brands are available – we use an excellent quality called Jivara made by Valrhona, our favourite brand.

For a rich chocolatey flavour, you need to use a brand with at least 60% cocoa solids. This will be indicated on the pack label – often emblazoned across the front as a large flash. I find that chocolate of 70% solids, although very fine, can be a bit too bitter for some of the mousses and when cold it will set a little too firm for my liking. For example, Dark and delicious chocolate torte (page 164) is best made with 60% solids so it remains moist and soft. White chocolate has no cocoa solids, hence its colour, but it does include vanilla and cocoa butter to give it a distinctive flavour and silky texture.

Chocolate making is quite an exact science. When we make our chocolates or dip ice cream balls into melted chocolate we like them to set to a sheen. This requires a process called tempering which can only be done effectively in a special machine that stirs the melted chocolate at a constant temperature. You can now buy domestic tempering machines – at a price and so strictly for the wealthy enthusiast.

Qualities of chocolate and their uses

• 70% and above cocoa solids is perfect where a bitter clean flavour is called for and our preferred type for making ganache. We use a quality called Guanaja.
• 60–55% cocoa solids – also known as couverture – is ideal for baked puddings and mousses, and for coating purposes.
• 40% cocoa solids – quality milk chocolate – is suitable for creamy mousses.
• White chocolate has no cocoa solids but good quality brands will taste deliciously creamy and are suitable for desserts and coating.

To melt chocolate

1 Break up the chocolate into a large heatproof bowl and stand this over a pan of very gently simmering water. Don't let the water get too hot, or allow it to come into contact with the chocolate, otherwise it will become overheated and seize.

2 Stir occasionally until melted and smooth, then immediately remove the bowl from the pan and allow the chocolate to cool.

• Alternatively, you can melt chocolate in the microwave. Break the chocolate into a suitable bowl and heat on High or Medium in 30 second bursts, stirring in between. A maximum of 2 minutes is probably sufficient for an average 150g bar, depending on the power wattage of your microwave oven.

• White chocolate is a little more tricky to melt and needs a more gentle heat. We often place it in a bowl on the edge of a warm stove to melt slowly over a period of a couple of hours.

• For a ganache, such as you would use for making truffles, I prefer to use hot cream to melt the chocolate. Simply break the chocolate into a bowl. Heat the cream until boiling, then slowly pour on to the chocolate, stirring in one direction until melted and smooth (illustrated below).

• Chocolate must be melted carefully to avoid overheating, which will cause it to seize. If you need to add alcohol, milk or water, then you must do so at the time of melting before you apply heat. If you add it after, again the chocolate might seize. If it seizes, chocolate turns into an unattractive thick, pasty lump. The only remedy is to try to dissolve the paste in some warm water, which then thins it down considerably.

Bitter chocolate truffles with wild honey

Truffles are quite simple to make, although they do take a little time to shape and coat. You start by making a rich ganache – a chocolate and cream mix – which is then chilled, shaped, coated in melted chocolate and given a final dusting of cocoa powder. You need two qualities of chocolate: bitter chocolate with 70% cocoa solids for the ganache; couverture or coating chocolate with 55–60% cocoa solids for dipping the truffles.

1 Put the double and single creams in a saucepan with the glucose and heat until boiling. Break up the dark chocolate and place in a heatproof bowl. Slowly pour on the hot cream, stirring in a circular movement in one direction only. Then mix in the warm honey in the same way. Stir the chocolate up from the base of the bowl to make sure everything is well mixed.

2 Allow the ganache to cool until it feels lightly warm (35–40°C), then mix in the diced butter, stirring until melted. Spoon the ganache out on to a plate and leave it to cool and firm up slightly, until it forms a slight crust on top.

3 For 'matchsticks' spoon the mixture into a piping bag fitted with a 1cm nozzle and pipe short lengths, about 5cm, on to a board. For balls, shape into rough spheres using a small teaspoon and roll them lightly in your hands; place on a plate. Chill the truffles until set.

4 Melt the couverture chocolate in a heatproof bowl over a pan of barely simmering water. To coat the balls or matchsticks, skewer one at a time with a thin satay stick or fine skewer and dip in the melted couverture. Then immediately toss in the sifted cocoa and set aside to firm. Keep chilled until ready to serve. Eat within 3–4 days.

Note: Concentrated butter is sold in some supermarkets. Otherwise you can clarify unsalted butter by melting it and carefully pouring off the melted butter fat into a bowl, leaving the milky deposits behind. Chill the butter fat before use.

MAKES ABOUT 500g

125ml double cream
25ml single cream
2 tablespoons liquid glucose
250g dark chocolate (about 70% cocoa solids)
65g clear wild or forest honey, warmed
65g concentrated butter, diced (see note)
about 125g couverture chocolate (55–60% cocoa solids)
cocoa powder, sifted, to finish

Chocolate truffle tartlets

MAKES ABOUT 24

1 quantity Chocolate Pastry (page 203)

GANACHE FILLING:

150ml milk

250ml double cream

250g dark chocolate (70% cocoa solids, such as
  Valrhona Guanaja)

These are ideal to serve as sweet canapés at a buffet. Make the chocolate pastry and bake the mini tart cases in advance, leaving the ganache filling to be piped in just before serving. You could also spoon in some Marinated cherries or Macerated fruits (page 13) before the ganache. Serve the tartlets at room temperature so the filling is soft.

1 Roll out the chocolate pastry on a lightly floured surface to a 5mm thickness. (As it's quite soft, use straight from the fridge.) Using a 6cm cutter, cut out 24 rounds and use to line two 12-hole small tartlet or bun tin trays. Prick the bases lightly with a fork and set aside to rest in a cool place for 20 minutes. Preheat the oven to 200°C, Gas 6.

2 Bake the tartlet cases blind for 10–12 minutes, pricking the bases if they rise. Leave in the tins for a few minutes to firm up, then carefully remove and transfer to a wire tray to crisp and cool completely.

3 Meanwhile, make the filling. Put the milk and half of the cream in a small pan and bring to the boil. Break the chocolate into a bowl. Pour on the hot cream mix and stir in one direction only until the chocolate is melted and the mixture is smooth. Cool until tepid.

4 Whip the remaining cream in a bowl until soft peaks form and fold into the ganache. Spoon into a piping bag fitted with a fluted nozzle and pipe into the tartlet cases. For an inviting glossy finish, wave a blow-torch over the tops, or flash under a piping hot grill for a few seconds.

Caramelised hazelnut chocolate clusters

MAKES ABOUT 24 CLUSTERS

200g caster sugar

1–2 tablespoons water

50g butter

100g whole hazelnuts

200g dark chocolate (55–60% cocoa solids)

Small clusters of nuts are set in a buttery caramel and then coated in melted chocolate. If preferred, you can use milk or white chocolate.

1 Line a baking sheet with a silicone cooking liner or baking parchment. Melt the sugar with the water in a heavy-based saucepan over a very gentle heat. Once all the sugar grains have dissolved, stir in the butter. Increase the heat and boil to a mid-golden colour. Take off the heat.

2 Drop in a cluster of 3 nuts, scoop out at once with a metal spoon and place on the lined baking sheet. Repeat with the remaining nuts to make about 24 clusters. Cool until set and firm.

3 Melt the chocolate (see page 183). Dunk each nut cluster into the chocolate to coat and place on baking parchment to set. Store in an airtight tin for up to 3 days.

White chocolate and strawberry ice balls

A sophisticated way of serving ice cream as petits fours. You will need cocktail sticks or satay sticks to skewer the ice balls for dipping.

1 After churning the strawberry ice cream, transfer to a shallow container and freeze until firm enough to shape into balls. Line 2 small freezerproof trays with baking parchment. Cover a block of polystyrene or florist's oasis with foil – this is to hold the ice balls upright as they set. (Failing this a pack of sugar will do.)
2 Using a melon baller – and working quickly – scoop the ice cream into small balls and place on the lined tray. Once you have shaped 6–8 balls, put the tray into the freezer so they don't melt. Continue like this, adding the ice cream balls to a tray and popping it back into the freezer as each batch of 6–8 is complete. Freeze until solid.
3 In the meantime, melt the white chocolate in a bowl over hot water (see page 183) and cool until barely tepid.
4 One at a time, skewer the ice cream balls on a stick and dip into the melted chocolate, swirling until coated. Push the stick into the block to hold it upright – the chocolate should set instantly to an even coating. Repeat quickly with the other balls.
5 Once set, remove the stick and coat the underside with chocolate, using your finger. Store in the freezer for up to a day before serving. Serve in little petits fours cases or skewered on the sticks.

MAKES 20–24
1 quantity Strawberry ice cream (page 58)
200g white chocolate

Chocolate truffle croquant

There is little to beat a light chocolate mousse served in small elegant glasses. This one is flavoured with my homemade honeycomb.

1 Break the chocolate into a large heatproof bowl. Reheat the crème anglaise until tepid and slowly pour on to the chocolate, stirring until melted. If necessary stand the bowl over a pan of gently simmering water. Cool to room temperature, stirring once or twice.
2 Whip the cream until softly stiff and fold into the cooled mixture. Crush the honeycomb in a food processor or blender to fine crumbs, then fold in.
3 Spoon or pipe into small wine glasses, using a piping bag fitted with a fluted nozzle. Serve at room temperature.

SERVES 8–12
½ quantity Crème anglaise (page 193)
300g dark chocolate (60% cocoa solids)
150ml double cream
100g Honeycomb (page 201)

basics

Crème anglaise

A great British classic, despite it's French name. Crème anglaise is the ultimate pouring sauce to serve with desserts; it is also the base for classic ice creams. I prefer to use UHT (longlife) milk because it seems to make the sauce more stable. Crème anglaise isn't difficult to make but you must cook it on the lowest possible heat, otherwise it will curdle. If you cook on gas, a heat diffuser is a good investment. A sugar thermometer can be used to check when it is cooked enough – the temperature should be 82°C.

MAKES ABOUT 600ml
250ml whole milk (preferably UHT)
250ml double cream
50g caster sugar
1–2 vanilla pods
6 large free-range egg yolks

1 Put the milk and cream in a heavy-based saucepan with 1 tablespoon of the sugar (to help prevent the liquid boiling over).
2 Holding the tip of the vanilla pod with your thumb, run the back of a knife along the length of the pod to flatten (this loosens the seeds). Keeping the tip end intact, slit the vanilla pod along its length and scoop out the tiny seeds with the tip of a knife.
3 Add the vanilla seeds to the pan, together with the empty pod(s) Slowly bring to the boil.
4 Meanwhile, using a balloon whisk, beat the egg yolks and remaining sugar together in a large bowl on a folded tea towel (to keep it steady) until pale and creamy.
5 When the liquid is on the point of boiling, pour about a third of it on to the egg mixture, whisking well. Gradually pour in the rest of the milk, whisking continuously.
6 Return this mixture to the pan, stirring. Cook on a very low heat, stirring continuously with a wooden spoon until it thickens slightly – enough to thinly coat the back of the spoon. If you draw a finger down the back of the spoon it should leave an impression
7 Immediately remove the pan from the heat and strain the custard through a fine sieve into a chilled bowl. Cover and allow to cool, stirring occasionally to prevent a skin forming. Chill until required. Crème anglaise can be refrigerated for 2–3 days but isn't suitable for freezing (unless churned into ice cream).

Minted crème anglaise
Omit the vanilla pod. Bring the creamy milk to the boil, then remove from the heat and add the leaves from 6 fresh mint sprigs. Set aside to infuse for 30 minutes, then discard the leaves and return to the boil. Continue as above.

Crème pâtissière

'Crème pat', as we affectionately call this, is the base for classic hot sweet soufflés; it also makes a wonderful filling for pastries and éclairs. Crème pâtissière must be smooth and cooked sufficiently to ensure the flour is properly cooked out – this allows you to incorporate the maximum amount of flavouring purée if you are making a hot soufflé. Most recipes call for about half this amount but it is easier to make a larger quantity – simply use half and refrigerate the rest for up to 2–3 days. UHT (longlife) milk makes for a more stable mixture.

1 Put the milk and cream in a heavy-based saucepan with 1 tablespoon of the sugar, the vanilla seeds and empty pod. Slowly bring to the boil.
2 Meanwhile, beat the egg, egg yolks and remaining sugar together in a large bowl with a balloon whisk until pale and creamy.
3 Sift a third of the cornflour into the bowl and whisk thoroughly, keeping the mixture smooth. Incorporate the rest of the cornflour in the same way (in two more goes).
4 When the creamy milk is on the point of boiling, pour a third on to the egg mixture, beating well. Gradually pour in the rest of the milk, whisking continuously. Take out the vanilla pod.
5 Return this mixture to the pan, whisking. Simmer gently for 3–4 minutes, whisking vigorously, until smooth and thick. You must ensure that the crème pat is properly cooked otherwise it will taste floury.
6 Pour into a bowl, cover and cool, then refrigerate until required.

MAKES ABOUT 650ml
350ml whole milk
150ml double cream
75g caster sugar
1 vanilla pod, slit lengthways and seeds extracted (see page 193)
1 large free-range egg
3 large free-range egg yolks
40g cornflour

MERINGUES

There are three great classic meringues in a pastry chef's repertoire – French, Italian and Swiss. The simplest is French meringue. For this, fine caster sugar is beaten into whisked egg whites until thick and glossy. The sugar must be whisked in thoroughly to ensure it dissolves into the egg whites and bakes without weeping. For most of the recipes in this book that call for meringue, this simple mixture will suffice, but it must be used immediately or it will break down. However, as chefs do not have time during service to whisk up meringue they prefer to use Italian meringue, which is made with a boiling sugar syrup, like pâte à bombe. This keeps for several hours in the fridge. (Swiss meringue is even stiffer – after beating the egg whites with the hot syrup, the mixture is beaten over a pan of simmering water for further stability.)

French meringue

MAKES ABOUT 500ml
2 large free-range egg whites, at room temperature
pinch of salt, or tiny squeeze of lemon juice
100g caster sugar

A quick and easy meringue to make and then bake immediately. This is the one to use for lemon meringue pie, or simple meringues that bake until crisp on the outside and chewy in the middle. It needs to be used within 10 minutes of making or it may start to break down.

1 Put the egg whites into a grease-free electric mixer, or large bowl if using a hand-held electric whisk. Add the salt or lemon juice and 1 tablespoon of the sugar. Beat slowly at first, then increase the speed to high. Beat until the foam forms soft peaks but do not over-whisk or the mixture will become dry and grainy.
2 Gradually whisk in the rest of the sugar, a tablespoon at a time.
3 Continue whisking until the meringue is smooth and glossy, and stands in firm peaks. Use as soon as possible.

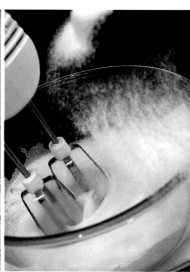

Italian meringue

The chefs' favourite meringue, this has a wonderful silky texture and stability, so it can be made in advance and stored in the fridge for up to 8 hours. Whisking a boiling sugar syrup (rather than caster sugar) into the whisked egg whites creates the stability. Don't be put off by the method – it really is very easy – all you need is a thermometer to check the temperature of the syrup. Liquid glucose is added to the syrup to stop the sugar crystallising.

1 Put the sugar, glucose and water in a small heavy-based saucepan and dissolve over a gentle heat, stirring once or twice. Once the sugar syrup is clear, increase the heat and place a sugar thermometer in the pan (if you have one).
2 Meanwhile, put the egg whites into a very clean bowl and whisk using an electric whisk to the soft peak stage.
3 Continue to boil the syrup until it reaches a temperature of 120°C, or the 'hard ball stage' when a little of the hot syrup dropped into a glass of cold water forms a firm, clear ball. This should take 5–7 minutes.
4 With the beaters working on slow speed, trickle the boiling syrup on to the beaten egg whites.
5 Continue whisking for about 5 minutes longer until the mixture is cooled to room temperature. Italian meringue should be silky smooth, stiff and brilliant white.

MAKES ABOUT 600ml
120g caster sugar
1 teaspoon liquid glucose
2 tablespoons water
2 large free-range egg whites

Pâte à bombe

MAKES 350ml
100ml water
150g caster sugar
5 large free-range egg yolks

This is used as the base for mousses and iced parfaits, which need a light stable foam of beaten egg yolks and sugar. A hot strong sugar solution is beaten into egg yolks, then whisked over a pan of simmering water to effectively 'cook' the foam and make it more stable. The sugar syrup must be boiled to the correct temperature – a sugar thermometer is useful to check this, but not essential. A small hand-held electric whisk is invaluable. You can store pâte à bombe for a day or two in the fridge, but give it another whip before use. It will freeze but should be whisked again once it has thawed and used immediately.

1 Put the water and sugar in a small heavy-based saucepan and heat slowly until dissolved and completely clear, stirring once or twice. Once the sugar syrup is clear, increase the heat and place a sugar thermometer in the pan (if you have one).

2 Meanwhile, whisk the egg yolks in a heatproof bowl using a hand-held electric mixer on full speed until pale yellow, thick and creamy.

3 Continue to boil the syrup until it reaches a temperature of 120°C, or the 'hard ball stage' when a little of the hot syrup dropped into a glass of cold water forms a firm, clear ball. This should take 5–7 minutes. Another good indication is when the syrup just begins to turn light caramel at the edges. As soon as the syrup reaches this stage, remove from the heat.

4 With the electric beaters still whirring, trickle the just-boiled syrup on to the whisked egg yolks (illustrated top right).

5 Carry on whisking with the mixer on full speed so the pâte à bombe increases in volume and becomes creamy (illustrated below left).

6 Once the mixture is a thick foam (illustrated below right), it may be used for ice creams and parfaits. However, for mousses you will need a thicker texture, so place the bowl over a pan of simmering water and whisk for a further 5 minutes until the mixture is thick and glossy, and stands in floppy round peaks. Remove the bowl from the heat and continue whisking until the mixture has cooled to room temperature; it should be softly stiff.

7 Use the pâte à bombe at room temperature or chill for up to 2 days, but make sure you whisk it again before use.

Stock syrup

MAKES ABOUT 750ml

500g granulated or caster sugar

500ml water

1 lemon

This is one of my great dessert basics. It is so useful to have in the fridge for dressing fresh fruit, poaching fruit or using in fruit terrines. We also dip wafer-thin fruit slices in this syrup prior to drying. You can flavour it as you like (see suggestions on page 10). In fact I suggest you keep some plain stock syrup and one flavoured version in the fridge. It keeps for up to 2–3 weeks.

The basic recipe is for a strong stock syrup; some recipes call for a light stock syrup (see below).

1 Put the sugar and water into a heavy-based saucepan and heat slowly until the sugar has dissolved. Stir once or twice during this time.
2 Meanwhile, using a swivel vegetable peeler, pare 3 strips of zest from the lemon and add these to the pan.
3 Once the sugar has dissolved, bring the syrup to the boil and boil for about 5 minutes.
4 Cool, then remove the zest strips and pour the syrup into a bottle or jar. (The lemon zest can be retained for a stronger flavour, but it does tend to colour the syrup yellow.)

Light stock syrup

You need to increase the proportion of water to sugar for a lighter stock syrup, so use 500ml per 250g sugar. (Makes about 625ml)

Alternatively, simply dilute the basic stock syrup with 250ml boiling water. (Makes about 1 litre)

My homemade honeycomb

This is basically a good old-fashioned caramel flavoured candy. If you like the centre of Crunchie bars, then you'll love it. It is rather like a light praline without the almonds. Crush it up and mix into ice cream or lemon sorbet, or sprinkle it over mousses and ices. Or simply break into chunks and munch as a treat.

MAKES ABOUT 400g
75g clear honey
140g jar liquid glucose
400g caster sugar
5 tablespoons water
20g bicarbonate of soda

1 Line a shallow baking tray with baking parchment. To loosen the honey and glucose, warm the jars in a pan of hot water so the contents flow easily. (To obtain the correct quantity, you can weigh a heavy-based saucepan on your scales and then pour in the warm syrups, adding the extra weights as necessary.)

2 Place the pan on a low heat and add the sugar and water. Heat, stirring occasionally, until the sugar dissolves.

3 Increase the heat to medium and cook until the syrup starts to turn a light golden caramel; it should register just under 150°C on a sugar thermometer. Mix in the bicarbonate of soda – it will foam like mad and look as if it's erupting. Immediately pour on to the prepared baking tray and allow it to flow level.

4 Set aside to cool for about 1 hour until firm and crisp, then break up into chunks.

5 If a recipe calls for crushed honeycomb, either whizz to the required texture in a food processor, or lightly pound in a bowl using the end of a rolling pin.

Pâte sucrée

MAKES ABOUT 1kg

250g butter, softened

180g caster sugar

3–4 vanilla pods

2 large free-range eggs, beaten

500g plain flour

¼ teaspoon fine sea salt

This is one of the standard pastries we use for tarts. Make up a big batch and divide into 3 or 4 portions. Wrap any portions that you don't need to use immediately in freezer film and freeze. For best results, make pâte sucrée in an electric mixer, then knead lightly by hand.

1 Using an electric mixer, beat the butter and sugar together in a bowl until smooth and creamy, but not fluffy. Slit open the vanilla pods and scrape out the seeds with the tip of a knife, adding them to the creamed mixture.

2 With the mixer on slow speed, gradually incorporate the beaten eggs. Stop the machine once or twice and scrape down the sides.

3 Sift the flour and salt together. With the mixer on its lowest speed, add the flour in 3 or 4 stages. As soon as the mixture comes together as a crumbly dough, stop the machine.

4 Gather the dough together and turn on to a lightly floured surface, preferably cool marble. Briefly knead it with your hands until smooth – this should only take a minute or two. Avoid over-working the pastry or it will become softened by the warmth of your hands.

5 Divide into 3 or 4 batches and wrap in cling film. Leave to rest in the refrigerator for 30 minutes before rolling out. Freeze any that you don't need now for later use.

6 Before you roll out pâte sucrée, give it another light kneading, to prevent it from cracking as you roll. Dust your work surface very lightly with flour and roll out the pastry quickly, using light, even strokes. If you apply too much pressure you will release the butter in the dough and it will be difficult to shape.

Fragrant orange pastry

Ring the changes with tarts and pies by varying the pastry instead of the filling. This one will light up your Christmas mince pies, or make a lemon tart extra heavenly. Alternatively, use it to make crisp tartlet cases – bake until crisp, cool then fill with whipped crème fraîche mixed with homemade lemon curd, and top with fresh strawberries. Fragrant orange pastry freezes well – most recipes call for half this amount so freeze the other half for another time. You will find orange flower water in the baking section of selected supermarkets and delicatessens.

MAKES ABOUT 450g
150g unsalted butter, softened
75g icing sugar, sifted
finely grated zest of 1 orange
2 free-range egg yolks, beaten
1 teaspoon orange flower water
250g plain flour

1 Beat the butter, icing sugar, orange zest, egg yolks and orange flower water together in a bowl to a soft cream.
2 Tip in the flour and mix with a table knife, then draw the mixture together with your hands and knead to a smooth dough.
3 Wrap in cling film and rest in the refrigerator for a good 2 hours. Give this pastry another light kneading before you roll it out – to prevent it from cracking.

Variation
For lemon pastry, omit the orange flower water and orange zest. Add the finely grated zest of 2 lemons and 1 teaspoon lemon juice instead.

Chocolate pastry

There are many uses for this pastry – not just chocolate tarts. It is perfect for lemon curd tartlets, and tiny cases to fill with strawberries and cream.

MAKES ABOUT 300g
125g plain flour
15g cocoa powder
$\frac{1}{2}$ teaspoon fine sea salt
60g caster sugar
60g butter, softened
30g dark chocolate, melted and cooled
1 free-range egg yolk

1 Sift the flour, cocoa powder and salt together.
2 In a large bowl, beat the sugar and butter together until pale and creamy, then beat in the melted and cooled chocolate.
3 Add the flour mixture and egg yolk and mix to a soft, smooth dough. Shape into a flattened ball, wrap in cling film and rest in the refrigerator for 30 minutes before rolling out.

Choux pastry

This is one of the easiest pastries to make – honest! You heat and beat everything together in a saucepan and then pipe – or spoon – the thick paste on to a greased baking sheet. The mixture rises to form crisp, light hollow dough balls, which can then be filled with whipped cream. My recipe includes a little condensed milk, which gives the pastry a sweet, crisp texture. Choux does soften if baked too far ahead, although this can be remedied with a brief reheat in a low oven.

1 Put the milk, water, condensed milk, salt and butter into a large heavy-based saucepan. Heat gently until the butter melts. Meanwhile, sift the flour.

2 Bring the liquid to a rolling boil, shoot the flour into the pan all at once and beat vigorously with a wooden spoon.

3 Keep beating the mixture over the heat until it comes together as a smooth, thick paste that leaves the side of the pan clean (illustrated below left).

4 Tip into a bowl and allow to cool for 5 minutes, then transfer to an electric mixer. With the mixer on a low speed, gradually work in the beaten eggs about a quarter at a time, increasing the speed to high between additions for 10 second bursts to aerate the mixture. Continue until you have a smooth paste, the texture of a stiff cake mix (shown right). Don't make it too soft – you may not need to add all of the egg.

5 Cool until the choux pastry is thick enough to spoon or pipe, but don't let it cool too much or it will be hard to shape.

MAKES 400g

5 tablespoons milk

5 tablespoons water

2 tablespoons sweetened condensed milk

$\frac{1}{2}$ teaspoon fine sea salt

70g butter, cut into small cubes

85g plain flour

3 medium free-range eggs, lightly beaten

All-butter puff pastry

MAKES 1.2kg

500g plain flour
¹⁄₂ teaspoon fine sea salt
500g butter, cut into chunks
1 teaspoon white wine vinegar
about 300ml ice-cold water

This is a robust puff, suitable for 'free standing' pastries such as Pithiviers (page 160).

1 Set aside 10g of the flour. Sift the rest of the flour and salt into a bowl and rub in 50g butter until the mixture looks like fine breadcrumbs. This can be done in a food processor.

2 Add the vinegar and gradually trickle in the ice-cold water, mixing with a table knife until it comes together as a smooth dough. You may not need all of the water, or you may need to add a little more. Wrap the dough in cling film.

3 Put the remaining 450g butter on a sheet of baking parchment and sprinkle with some of the reserved flour. Place another sheet of baking parchment on top and pat out to a rectangle, measuring 23 x 33cm, lifting the paper and sprinkling with flour as you do so. Chill until firm; refrigerate the dough at the same time, for about 20 minutes.

4 On a lightly floured surface, roll out the dough to a 25 x 35cm rectangle, slightly larger than the dimensions of the butter, keeping your knuckles under the rolling pin to ensure you apply an even pressure (illustrated below left). Make sure the edges and corners are straight and neat – one of the secrets of success. If necessary, tease the dough into shape.

5 Place the chilled butter rectangle on top of the rolled dough, leaving a margin at the edges (shown opposite, top left). Fold in two, enclosing the butter. Press the dough edges together well to seal in the butter.

6 Pat out the dough evenly, with your knuckles under the rolling pin to keep the pressure even (illustrated top right). Then roll out the dough in one direction only until it is three times the length, making sure none of the butter breaks through.

7 Fold the dough in three, bringing the top third down to the centre then folding the bottom third on top (shown opposite, bottom left).

8 Give the dough a quarter turn and roll out as before always in the same direction, lightly dusting with flour as necessary. Fold as before, keeping those edges neat (illustrated bottom right), then wrap in cling film and chill for 20 minutes, or longer in warm weather.

9 Unwrap with the fold to the same side as before and roll out for a third time. Fold as before, that is top to centre then bottom over; this is known as a 'simple fold'. Then fold this in half again, like a wallet; this we call a 'double fold'. Wrap and chill for 20 minutes. Finally, divide into portions as dictated by your recipe.

Mascarpone flaky pastry

MAKES ABOUT 1.4kg

BUTTERY MIXTURE:

200g mascarpone

250g butter, softened

50g strong plain flour

FLOURY DOUGH:

500g strong plain flour

1 teaspoon fine sea salt

50g butter, melted and cooled

400ml water

This is a lovely light and tender pastry with a melt-in-the-mouth texture. It is made by rolling a buttery mascarpone mixture into a floury dough. As you roll the two into each other, you incorporate the fat into the flour in thin layers, which is what makes this rich pastry rise in flaky layers. It isn't easy to make a small amount, so I suggest you make this large quantity, divide it into 4 portions (each about 350g) and freeze what you don't need.

1 For the buttery mixture, beat the mascarpone with the softened butter and flour. Shape into a small square and wrap in cling film.

2 To make the floury dough, sift the flour and salt together into a bowl, add the runny butter and water then mix to a firm dough. Knead firmly for 5 minutes or so, until smooth and elastic. Shape into a square, about 2cm thick, and wrap in cling film. Chill both doughs for 6 hours.

3 Unwrap both the buttery slab and the floury dough. Score a deep cross on top of the floury dough in the centre, cutting about halfway through the depth. Pull back the 4 points of dough at the centre of the cross and position the slab of butter in the centre at an angle (illustrated left).

4 Fold the pointed ends of the dough back into the centre over the butter to enclose it (illustrated bottom left).

5 Roll the 2 doughs together lightly but firmly on a lightly floured board until 2 to 3 times the length, and about 1.5cm thick. Keep the edges straight and make sure none of the butter breaks through.

Fold the dough in three, bringing the top third down to the centre then folding the bottom third on top. This is known as a 'simple fold'. (Techniques as illustrated for All-butter puff pastry, page 206–7). Wrap in cling film and rest in the refrigerator for 20–30 minutes until firm.

6 Give the dough a quarter turn, so the fold is either on the right or left. Roll out and fold again, then quarter turn so the fold is on the same side as before.

7 Roll out the pastry a third time, to the same length as before. Fold as before, that is top to centre then bottom over. Then fold this in half again, like a wallet, to make a 'double fold'. Wrap and chill until firm.

8 Roll out and fold again, making sure the fold is on the same side as before. All these stages are necessary if the layers of fat are to be evenly distributed throughout the flour and the pastry is to rise evenly.

9 Roll out for a final time and make a 'simple fold'. Wrap and chill. Cut the dough into 4 portions (or the quantities required), and freeze those you don't need straightaway.

Minute puff pastry

Make this feuilletage when you want a quick, light flaky pastry in minutes. You simply mix, knead, roll and fold – that's all. Don't expect the high rise that you get with All-butter puff or Mascarpone flaky pastry, but you will certainly have a pastry that is flaky and buttery. It's wonderful for fruit tarts and apple pies.

MAKES 700g
250g strong plain flour
¹/₂ teaspoon fine sea salt
250g butter, at room temperature but not soft
about 150ml cold water

1 Sift the flour and salt into a large bowl. Cut the butter into small dice and mix into the flour (illustrated above left); don't rub it in.
2 Gradually mix in enough cold water to give a rough dough that is firm, not sticky. Use the back of a wooden spoon to do this rather than your hands – to keep the pastry cool (illustrated above centre).
3 Finally, gather the dough together with your hand (illustrated above right). Cover with cling film and rest in the fridge for 20 minutes.
4 Turn the dough out on to a lightly floured board and knead gently until smooth, shaping it to a rectangle. Roll out in one direction only until it is approximately 15 x 50cm. Make sure the edges remain straight and even.
5 Fold the dough in three, bringing the top third down to the centre, then folding the bottom third on top. Give the dough a quarter turn to the left or right and roll out again to 3 times the length. Fold the pastry as before, cover with cling film and chill for at least 30 minutes before rolling out to use.

Brioche loaf

MAKES 2 LARGE LOAVES

500g strong plain bread flour

1 sachet easy-blend yeast

1 teaspoon fine sea salt

2 tablespoons caster sugar

6 medium free-range eggs, beaten

240g butter, softened

1 egg yolk, beaten with 1 teaspoon cold water
to glaze

Homemade brioche is a revelation. It has a wonderful flavour, and can be made less sweet than shop-bought brioche. We toast brioche slices to serve with starters, but it is also perfect for summer puddings and bread puddings. The recipe uses easy-blend yeast, as it is easy to obtain. If you can find fresh yeast, use it instead – cream 15g with 2 tablespoons tepid milk and add with the beaten eggs. Brioche is a very rich dough and consequently takes longer to rise than ordinary bread.

1 Lightly warm an electric mixer bowl. Tip in the flour, yeast, salt and sugar and mix gently until evenly combined. With the machine on low speed, gradually mix in the beaten eggs until smooth.

2 With the mixer still on low speed, add the butter a spoonful at a time. Once all the butter has been incorporated, mix for a further 10 minutes.

3 Cover the bowl and leave in a warm place, such as an airing cupboard, until the dough has doubled in size (illustrated top left). In the meantime, grease and flour two 900g loaf tins or terrines.

4 Knock back the risen dough by beating with a wooden spoon (illustrated top right) and then divide in half. Cut each portion into three and roll into balls, using floured hands. Place in the prepared tins and press lightly. Cover with cling film and leave to prove in a warm place until risen to three-quarters fill the tins, 1–3 hours. This second rising is vital for light-textured brioche.

5 Meanwhile, preheat the oven to 190°C, Gas 5. Remove the cling film and brush the brioche loaves with the egg glaze. Bake for 30–35 minutes until risen and golden. Leave in the tins for 5 minutes, then turn out and cool completely on a wire rack. Use within a day or two, or freeze well wrapped and use within 6 weeks.

reference

Ingredients

FLOURS

We use two types of plain white flour: a soft, all-purpose plain flour (type 45) for cakes and some pastries; and a strong plain or bread flour (type 55) that is high in gluten and best for certain pastries, yeast doughs and some batters. Rice flour is lighter and better for tempura-style batters – you can buy it from Oriental stores. Note that ground rice isn't the same product. Cornflour (maize flour) is gluten free and sometimes mixed with plain flour to make it softer. It may also be used to thicken light sauces. Arrowroot and potato flour can be used to make clear glazes for flans.

SUGARS

Caster sugar is the most useful refined sugar for desserts because it dissolves quickly when beaten with eggs or butter. Granulated sugar isn't suitable for whisking or creaming because it remains gritty, but it is fine for making syrups, jams and jellies. Less refined 'golden caster' and 'golden granulated' both have an agreeable light caramel flavour – good in syrups for fruit salads – but they do not dissolve as well as their refined counterparts. Where a richer flavour is called for – in some sticky puddings – I like to use unrefined light muscovado sugar. This doesn't cream as well for mousses or light cakes, but it can be used half and half with caster sugar.

Flower scented honeys will enhance ice creams, flavoured stock syrups and roasted fruits, but they should be used half and half with sugar, otherwise their fragrance may overpower a dessert. Acacia, thyme and orange flower honeys are my favourites.

FATS

To my mind, there is no substitute for the flavour or texture of butter. We use Normandy or Dutch butter – both unsalted and lightly salted. If a recipe calls for softened butter, remember to take it from the fridge the night before, or well in advance. I find a chilled pack of butter takes 4–6 hours to reach the right consistency for creaming. If you forget, then cut it into small cubes, place in a bowl and blitz for a few seconds in the microwave – on low so it doesn't actually melt. I grease cake tins and soufflé dishes with softened butter (see page 98) but you can use a bland oil, such as sunflower, if you prefer.

Some of my cake recipes call for browned butter, which imparts a deliciously nutty flavour. This is made by heating melted butter until just turning golden brown, then straining it through muslin to remove the solids. The fat is then cooled to room temperature before use. Clarified butter is made in the same way, but without the browning.

MILK AND CREAM PRODUCTS

Cream is available in a range of differing fat contents, from thin pouring cream to ultra thick clotted cream. Double cream, with a butterfat content of 48%, is the type we use most often. It can be whipped easily to hold firm but soft peaks – perfect for folding into cold desserts. With a fat content of 35%, whipping cream is lighter and ideal for crème chantilly or soft, creamy desserts but it is not good for my mousses or ices. Single cream, with a fat content of 18%, is suitable to serve as a light pouring cream. Soured cream has the same fat content as single cream and is sometimes used in cheesecakes.

Crème fraîche has the same fat content as double cream and although it appears set in the tub, it can also be whipped. Reduced fat crème fraîche is more suitable for spooning or pouring.

Thick Greek yogurt contains around 10% fat and lends a rich creamy taste to desserts. Natural yogurt may be anything from 5% to almost fat free. Fromage frais can be spooned on top of compotes and hot roasted fruits to add a light tangy richness. It comes in two fat levels – 8% and close to 0%. However if fromage frais is to be heated, it must be stabilised with a little flour or egg yolk to prevent it from curdling.

Where a recipe calls for milk, I generally use whole (full-fat) milk, but you'll note that some of my recipes – custards and crème brûlées – call for UHT (long-life) whole milk. I find this is more stable in cooking – perhaps because it's been heat treated, which stabilises the fat.

Equipment

Desserts and pâtisserie are quite exact forms of cooking. Whilst there is scope for spontaneous creativity, say with fruit salads or roasted fruits, for recipes that require measuring, specific culinary techniques and temperature control it helps to have the right tools. Most of the tools we use are of a professional quality and endure many years. My advice would be to buy the best quality equipment you can afford because it lasts and lasts.

WEIGHING AND MEASURING

Careful weighing is important for baking – we use battery operated digital scales for accurate measurements of small quantities. Otherwise, I suggest traditional balance scales with a set of metric weights ranging from 5g to 2kg. If you are still using imperial weights, do invest in a set of metric ones – it is far easier to weigh in metric than convert recipes to imperial. Spring balance scales are to be avoided – they are neither accurate, nor easy-to-read in small units.

Timings are given in recipes but as many extraneous factors are involved and no two cooks (or chefs) work in the same way, these can only ever be approximate. An accurate thermometer takes away the guesswork. A sugar thermometer is a must if you intend to make pâte à bombe, Italian meringue, stock syrup, caramel etc. It is also invaluable for sauces such as crème anglaise – a couple of seconds either way can mean the difference between velvety smooth custard and a curdled disaster. Ovens are notoriously variable and while it's useful to have an oven thermometer, I feel it is more important to get to know your own oven. My recipe timings are given as guidelines, with descriptions of colour and texture as back up.

BAKING TINS AND MOULDS

One extravagance I would advise is the best quality metal baking sheets you can afford. These do need to be heavy to conduct heat evenly during baking, but you will also find them useful to lay on certain biscuits during cooling to keep them flat. Similarly a heavy baking sheet is important when it forms the base for a flan ring. Even when you are baking a flan case blind in a flan tin, you should place the tin on a heavy metal sheet to promote base cooking. And I would suggest you have at least three baking sheets, so you can easily bake cookies, tuiles etc in batches.

Metal cake tins and moulds must not buckle or bend (we use the Bourgeat brand). Rather than wash these after every use, we prefer to wipe them whilst still hot with a damp cloth, so they build up a natural non-stick patina. Springform tins (loose based with sides that can be clicked to lock and unlock) are ideal for light soft cakes and cheesecakes, and a range of these in different sizes will prove useful. If you often make sponges you might like to buy one or two moule à manque tins – special cake tins with gently sloping sides. Loaf tins for bread can double as moulds for parfaits and fruit terrines and vice versa, you can bake loaves in terrines. Savarin rings and Kugelhopf moulds can be used for almost any cake mixture. For brioche you can buy traditional tins with fluted sloping sides, but we often use loaf tins for large brioche and muffin tins for individual ones. Dariole moulds too, can be used for individual cakes and bavarois.

Jelly moulds come in many shapes and sizes – the most useful is a 1 litre size. Ornate metal or plastic moulds may be attractive for jellies and bavarois but we prefer to use porcelain terrine moulds because they don't overheat when dipped into boiling water to demould.

LINERS

Many of the recipes in this book require non-stick liners. Baking parchment is widely available and adequate for lining cake tins and baking sheets for cakes, cookies, small chocolates etc, but not for drying out wet mixtures like syrup-dipped fruits. For these, non-stick silicone liners are better. Sold under the names of Silpat, Teflon Cake Liners, Bake-o-Glide or Magic Carpet, these coated re-usable mats last for months, even years, requiring just a quick wipe with a hot cloth to keep them clean.

BOWLS, WHISKS AND SIEVES

Mixing bowls should be wide enough to facilitate whisking. You will need a selection of sizes. We do use glass bowls, but for whisking egg white and cream by hand we often employ round-bottomed stainless steel bowls as they ensure all the contents are reached by the whisk. These bowls also fit snugly into a saucepan when you need to whisk over hot water. A balloon whisk is best for incorporating air into a mixture by hand, but for many purposes it is more convenient to use a free-standing or hand-held electric whisk. These are thorough and take the effort out of whisking, but as they work fast you need to watch them all the time.

Fine rounded sieves are essential for sifting flours with raising agents, and dusting with icing sugar and cocoa powder. Fine-meshed conical sieves are a better option for sauces, such as crème anglaise, to ensure a perfectly smooth texture. Use a medium-mesh sieve when you are instructed to rub a purée through a sieve with the back of a ladle. For clear jellies and liquids we often line the sieve with butter muslin before straining. You can buy this by the metre from the fabric section of department stores.

PASTRY TOOLS

My rich, buttery, soft pastry doughs are best rolled on marble slabs that keep their cool. As these are porous and absorb flavours, it's best to keep one solely for the purpose. It's also worth investing in a good hardwood rolling pin – a simple, long cylinder without handles for even pressure. Pastry brushes are needed for greasing bowls and moulds, as well as brushing excess flour from pastry, and applying glazes to tarts, pies etc. I suggest you have at least three – actually, we find small decorator's brushes are better for most tasks. Pastry chefs swear by their flexible plastic pastry scrapers, which effectively clean mixtures from cake tins and bowls. Similarly cake spatulas should be very bendy too.

KNIVES AND CUTTING TOOLS

Serrated fruit knives are needed for segmenting oranges and slicing apples and pears. Flexible palette knives are a must, especially medium to small sizes. These are the best tools for sliding cookies and tuiles off baking sheets, and for levelling the tops of soufflés and mousses. A mandolin is perfect for cutting wafer-thin slices of firm fruits, which

we dip in sugar syrup and dry until crisp. The Japanese brands are excellent.

A selection of plain pastry cutters is most useful, especially in the 5–7cm range. We use these to mould desserts for attractive presentation, as well as for cutting out pastry rounds. Our cutters are made by Matpher and can be bought from professional kitchen equipment stores.

SMALL APPLIANCES

There are a few useful small electric appliances you might like to invest in. For almost instant blending and frothing there is nothing to beat a chef's best friend, the Bamix stick blender. We are hard on ours, but there are domestic brands for less intensive use. A food processor or free-standing blender can be used for puréeing and blending instead. A sturdy, light hand-held electric mixer is ideal for whisking eggs and hot syrup for pâte à bombe, Italian meringue and small amounts of cream. A free-standing mixer is useful provided you have space for one on a work surface. If you enjoy homemade ices, an ice cream machine that churns as it freezes will reward you with smooth creamy textured ices and sorbets – well worth the expense especially if you entertain a lot.

USEFUL SUPPLIERS

Many chic kitchen shops and departmental stores sell designer pans, pots, dishes and small equipment, but the durability of these items is rarely as good as those found in professional stores. Some of these have retail outlets, stocking items in domestic sizes.

Stores include *Hansens* 304–306 Fulham Road, London SW10 (020 7351 6933); *Divertimenti* 139–141 Fulham Road, London SW3 (020 7581 8065) and 45–47 Wigmore Street, London W1 (020 7935 0689); *Pages* 121 Shaftesbury Avenue, London WC2; *David Mellor* 4 Sloane Square, London SW1 (0207 730 4259) and The Round Building, Hathersage, Sheffield (01433 650220).

For mail order supplies you can contact *Continental Chef Supplies* (0191 526 4107, or www.chefs.co.uk); *Scott & Sargeant* (0845 601 2815, or www.scottsargeant.com); *Cucina Direct* (0870 727 4300, or www.cucinadirect.co.uk); *David Mellor* (0207 730 4259, or davidmellordesign.com).

Glossary of culinary terms

BAIN-MARIE A water bath in which a dish is cooked to moderate the temperature so the mixture does not overcook or curdle, and the sides do not become crusty. In the oven a roasting tin half filled with boiling water serves as a bain-marie. On top of the stove, the mixture is placed in a heatproof bowl containing 5–7cm gently simmering water.

BAKING BEANS Dried pulses such as lentils or beans used to weigh down pastry during baking blind. Ceramic baking beans are also available.

BAKING BLIND To bake an unfilled pastry flan case until cooked and crisp. The pastry dough is pressed into a flan tin, or flan ring on a baking sheet, covered with foil or baking parchment and filled with baking beans to stop it from rising. (Illustrated on page 122.)

BASTE To spoon the pan juices or a syrup over foods such as roasted fruit during cooking to keep them moist and encourage them to caramelise.

BIND To mix liquid such as beaten egg or water into pastry or other dry mixture to bring it together.

BLANCH To dip uncooked food into boiling water, syrup or hot oil very briefly to seal the outside or semi-cook it. This may take less than a minute, a few minutes at the most. The food is then refreshed (see right).

BRULEE Literally translated as 'burnt' this term describes a cream-based sweet, sprinkled with an even layer of demerara or caster sugar, then caramelised – either with a blow-torch or under a very hot grill.

BRUNOISE Very finely diced fruits.

CARAMELISE To heat melted sugar or sugar syrup until it colours and forms a caramel. Also applies to food cooked in a hot dry pan so the natural sugars brown, enhancing the flavour. Sometimes fruits are brushed with softened butter and tossed in sugar first, to help the process.

CONFIT Fruits cooked very slowly submerged in syrup then served 'on the side' as a type of sweet relish. We confit the zest of citrus fruit to serve alongside tarts. Submerged in the syrup, this keeps for a good 2–3 months in the fridge.

COULIS A smooth fruit sauce made with a fruit purée and stock syrup.

CURDLE Inadvertently, certain sauces and creamed mixtures can be separated by overheating, or mixing with acidic foods. Curdling is due to the proteins in cream or eggs coagulating and forming small lumps. To avoid this happening, heat sensitive mixtures should be heated carefully and not allowed to boil. Alternatively, they may be stabilised with starch such as cornflour.

DECANT To pour one liquid from a bottle into another bottle or jug. This is done slowly so any sediment in the base of the bottle is left behind and can be discarded.

DEGLAZE To pour a little alcohol or other liquid into a hot pan and stir vigorously to soften any residue and mix with the pan juices so they may be used for a sauce. The liquid evaporates away a little to concentrate the flavour. For example, a shot of wine may be used to deglaze a pan in which fruit has been caramelised with butter and sugar.

DUST To lightly sprinkle with icing sugar, flour, cocoa powder or ground spice, shaking from a fine sieve.

FILO A wafer-thin pastry dough that has been pulled into thin sheets, rather than rolled – sold in packets or boxes. It is assembled in layers with melted butter or oil. Filo must be kept covered to prevent it drying out.

FLAMBE To ignite a mixture containing alcohol – usually in a sauté pan – to burn off the alcohol, concentrating and mellowing the flavour.

FOLDING IN To combine at least two mixtures gently together with a large metal spoon to retain the light texture. The spoon is turned gently in a figure-of-eight action so that it scoops up and gently incorporates mixture from the base of the bowl. Usually one of the mixtures is whipped egg whites or cream.

GLAZE To apply a coating to food before or after cooking for an attractive shiny finish. Fruit may be glazed with coulis or sugar syrup. Pastry and bread are often glazed with beaten egg.

INFUSE To immerse flavouring ingredients – such as herbs, citrus zest or vanilla pods – in hot syrup, milk or other liquid to impart a subtle flavour and aroma. The flavourings are usually added to the just-boiled liquid and left to stand for a while before being removed.

JULIENNE Very thinly sliced strips of citrus fruit zest or leafy herbs.

JUS The pure extracted juice of fruit without additional water or syrup. We extract pure strawberry jus from berries over a bain-marie for example, and make an apple jus by sieving puréed fresh (uncooked) apples.

KNEAD To work a dough by hand on a lightly floured board. Most pastries are given a light kneading to make them smooth before rolling out. Yeast doughs are kneaded more vigorously using the heel of the hand and a pummelling action to strengthen and develop the gluten.

LET DOWN To thin a liquid or mixture with a thinner one.

MACERATE To steep fruits in a liquid, usually syrup or alcohol, to flavour and soften them.

MI-CUIT Dried fruits, such as prunes or apricots, that have been partially cooked so they do not necessarily require soaking before use.

PARE To thinly peel the skin or zest from fruit, using a small, sharp knife or vegetable peeler.

PECTIN A carbohydrate present in fruit – especially acidic fruits – that forms a set when combined and heated with sugar.

POACH To cook food in a liquid that is kept just below boiling point. The liquid should barely bubble. For example, fruit may be poached in a light stock syrup so that it remains whole.

PROVE The second rising of a yeast dough, after knocking back and shaping.

PUREE To blend or sieve food, such as fruit, to a smooth pulp. Soft berry fruits and bananas can be puréed raw, other fruits may need to be cooked lightly to soften them first.

REDUCE To boil liquid, such as fruit juice, in an uncovered wide pan to evaporate some of the water and concentrate the flavour.

REFRESH To place food that has been just blanched into ice-cold water to stop any further cooking and bring down the temperature rapidly.

RIBBON STAGE Whisking egg yolks and sugar, often over a bain-marie, until the mixture forms a foam that is thick enough to leave a trail when some of the mixture is lifted up on the whisk and falls back into the bowl.

SCALDING POINT To bring milk and/or cream to just below boiling point. Scalding point is reached once the liquid starts to froth around the edge of the pan, just before it starts to creep up. At this stage take it off the heat immediately.

STEEP To soak ingredients in liquid, usually to soften them.

STRAIN To pass a liquid through a sieve to make sure it is entirely free of tiny particles. Sometimes it is necessary to rub the liquid through the sieve using the back of a ladle.

WHIPPING Incorporating air into an ingredient or mixture by beating rapidly with a balloon whisk or electric whisk. Ingredients such as cream and egg whites may be whipped to various stages – lightly thickened, softly stiff, or stiff peaks, for example. Three-quarters whipped cream that is whipped until thickened and forms light soft floppy peaks is a good texture for folding into mousses.

Wines to accompany desserts

By the time you reach the dessert course of a formal meal you may feel that having a glass of sweet wine is nothing short of overkill. But in fact a small glass of well chosen, sweet wine can really enhance a pudding. Finicky sommeliers prefer the term 'sweet' to 'dessert' because it implies that these wines needn't be restricted to puddings. Sweet wines are a diverse group so it helps to have some knowledge of their different styles – red through to white, sparkling and still, heavy or light, high or low in alcohol.

SWEET WINES OF THE WORLD

Many wine-producing countries – from France to Romania and Hungary – have been making delicious and complex sweet wines for centuries. As with all wines, the grape variety, viti and viniculture determine the flavour, body and character. For some sweet wines, the grapes are left on the vine to ripen later and develop a special fungal rot known as *botrytis cinerea* or 'noble rot'. This causes the grapes to shrivel and natural sugars to intensify.

France produces some of the most famous sweet wines. The best known come from Sauternes in the Bordeaux region, with famous names such as Barsac, Cadillac and Cérons, and south of Bordeaux from Monbazillac in Bergerac, and Jurançon in the foothills of the Pyrenees. Noble rot of the *sémillon* grape is challenging for the grower because not all of the grapes shrivel at the same time, even on the same bunch. Pickers are sometimes forced to use tweezers to extract each precious berry. Generally the wines from here will develop a rich golden colour and a citrus flavour, reminiscent of orange marmalade. Further north in the Loire valley, in Coteaux-du-Layon, Bonnezeaux and Quarts-de-Chaume, the *chenin blanc* grape produces wines with a lighter, fresher style plus hints of pineapple and honey.

Alsace on the German border is the home of the *gewürztraminer* and *tokay pinot gris* grapes. Wines produced from these grapes have a rich, spicy complexity – good not only with desserts, but also foie gras and pâtés. With Alsace wines it helps to know a little label language. VT or *vendange tardive* is wine from late picked grapes and implies more sweetness and/or strength. The lighter style SGN *sélection des grains nobles* are produced from hand sorted, well ripened grapes and possess a fine flavour.

Sweet, nutty *vin de paille* (straw wine) can be found in the Rhone Valley – grapes are dried on straw to concentrate the natural sugars. Further south are the *vin doux naturels* – wines that have had their natural fermentation halted with added grape spirit. These include favourites such as Muscat de Beaumes-de-Venise and Muscat de Lunel, and the heavier port like wines of Banyuls and Maury.

Spain produces sweet wines from the *pedro ximénez* (PX) grapes, in the form of heavy, luscious sherries. Jerez de la Frontera is famous for sherry and similar styles emerge from Malaga and Madeira. These deep coloured, viscous wines are packed with aromas of nuts, caramel and raisins. They contrast with the lighter citrus Moscatel de Valencia from Spain's eastern coast. Portugal is, of course, renowned for port – the classic fortified sweet wine with rich, concentrated black fruit aroma and high alcohol.

Italy gives us the famous *vin santo* or 'holy wines' of Tuscany, whilst the fine Recioto wines of Verona are pressed from late picked, straw dried grapes and develop floral, spicy flavours with aromas of peach and orange.

Germany and Austria produce some fabulous sweet wines. The best are from the versatile *riesling* grape offering a great range of flavours, from very delicate floral bouquets with light apple and honeysuckle tones, through to more intense flavours with hints of exotic mango and pineapple. Gothic German wine labels look confusing, so it helps to understand the terminology. *Auslese*, produced from specially selected bunches, are lightly sweet wines; *beerenauslese* (BA) are wines from over-ripe bunches; *trockenbeerenauslese* (TBA) are made from grapes affected by noble rot; the ultimate *Eiswein* are wines from grapes picked and crushed whilst still frozen.

Many wine merchants stock sweet wines from other parts of the world too. In Eastern Europe there are sweet wine making traditions as old as those of Bordeaux. The most famous is Hungarian Tokaji, a unique wine, highly prized for centuries by connoisseurs for its distinctive complex aromas of caramel, orange confit and dried banana. Cyprus produces the intensely sweet Commandaria of St. John, from sun-dried grapes. Sicily is famous for Marsala wines that are destined not just for sipping but also for flavouring desserts like zabaglione and trifles.

South Africa is home to the sweet wine, Constantia, which at one time was more in demand than Sauternes. Devotees of Australian wine might like to sip the thick and heavy liqueur muscats of Rutherglen and Mudgee, or the *botrytis* wines of New Zealand. In America, Californian wine makers produce excellent sweet Rieslings and Black Muscats. Even the Canadians are taking advantage of their crisp climate to make some notable ice wines.

MATCHING SWEET WINES AND DESSERTS

When you come to choosing a sweet wine for a meal, consider the sweetness levels of both dessert and wine. A light wine served with a rich dessert will generally taste thin and watery. Conversely a very fruity dish usually benefits from a wine of high acidity. But this principle doesn't always follow, so be prepared to experiment. For example a light and semi-sparkling Moscato or Prosecco will have a refreshing palate-cleansing effect on a heavy sponge fruit pudding. That said, the following general guidelines apply.

Fruit salads Choose wines made from *riesling* or *chenin blanc* grapes with high fruit acidity. Try German wines of at least *auslese* level, Loire valley wines, sweet Australian Rieslings and Jurançons. Recioto di Soave is a good match for desserts with oranges or bananas. If the fruit salad includes a spicy syrup or infusion of herbs like basil, then consider Alsace Gewürztraminers (SGN level) or a fortified Muscat from the south of France. If you are making the fruit salad yourself, macerate the fruit in a little of the wine first, to give it a kick start for a perfect match. If a fruit dessert, such as a jelly, is flavoured with a liqueur like Malibu, serve an extra shot alongside.

Sorbets and ices The subtle nuances of a sweet wine can be masked by low temperatures so it is best to serve full flavoured wines that retain character when chilled. For the classic chocolate/orange combination try orangey Muscats with chocolate ice creams. Apple scented Loire wines are excellent with light caramel or cinnamon ice cream, while classic vanilla ice cream is divine with a good shot of heavy PX sherry trickled over. Well chilled sparkling wines with good acidity are great with fruit sorbets, but not creamy ices. Or complement a sorbet with an appropriate fruit eau-de-vie such as pear, strawberry, quince, apricot or raspberry – even a glass of Calvados with apple sorbet.

Creamy mousses Sparkling wines score well with these desserts too. A light, frothy textured dessert is fabulous served with an Italian Moscato d'Asti from Piedmont, or demi-sec Loire Moelleux, while a richer Aussie sparkler is better with a tropical mango mousse. To accompany a chocolate mousse, pour small glasses of a rich fortified Bual from Madeira.

Chocolate desserts These are sometimes thought to be tricky to match with wine because chocolate has a heavy coating effect on the palate, but accept the challenge and try less traditional choices. Lighter milk and white chocolate puddings are good with floral Muscats such as Rivesaltes, Lunel or Beaumes-de-Venise from the south of France. Heavier dark chocolate desserts suit fortified wines – sherry, Madeira and late bottled vintage (LBV) ports. Alternatively, serve Hungarian Tokaji, Australian Rutherglen or Californian Black Muscat. For chocolate and orange desserts choose Monbazillac or Saussignac from Bordeaux, and if the dessert contains a liqueur then serve a matching shot alongside. At Christmas serve chestnut and chocolate desserts with French Pineau des Charentes, a grape juice fortified with Cognac.

Caramels and butterscotch These flavours go well with sweet wines, especially those made with noble rot grapes. Sauternes from the big '83 vintages with lots of *botrytis* and orange marmalade tones are wonderful with simple crème caramels, as are Hungarian Tokaji and Italian *vin santo*.

Christmas This is an excuse to indulge in some of the big sticky wines that highlight all those wonderful flavours of spices, dried fruits and nuts – Oloroso sherries sweetened with PX grapes, LBV ports, bual Maderia, dulce Malaga, as well as the great classic sweet wines of the world.

On a final note, some of the world's finest sweet wines are best drunk as a dessert in themselves. Any food, for example, must surely take second place to a bottle of Château d'Yquem '67!

Index

A

all-butter puff pastry, 206

almonds: almond and cherry
 Pithiviers, 160

 cherry and almond clafoutis,
 115

 espresso coffee and roasted
 almond bavarois, 97

 financiers, 173

 lemon and almond madeleines,
 178

 nut tuiles, 170

 roasted almond cream, 52

 vanilla macaroons, 176

angelica ice cream, 61

apples: apple and cranberry
 compote, 16

 apple coulis, 12

 baked apples with peppercorns,
 37

 deep-dish autumn fruit pie, 143

 golden apple streusel tart, 136

 green apple and grapefruit
 bavarois, 94

 green apple sorbet, 77

 roasted rhubarb and apple
 crumble, 129

apricots: apricot and cinnamon
 mousse, 91

 apricot and passion fruit
 bavarois, 93

 apricot compote, 14

 glazed apricots, 43

Armagnac: prune and Armagnac
 custard tart, 123

 prune and Armagnac ice cream,
 63

B

babas, rum, 119

baby meringues, 179

baguette and butter pudding laced
 with Baileys, 126

Baileys cream liqueur: baguette
 and butter pudding laced with
 Baileys, 126

 Baileys ice cream, 58

bain marie, 216

baking beans, 216

baking blind, 216

baking parchment, 214

baking sheets, 214

baking tins, 214

balloon whisks, 215

balsamic vinegar: roasted black
 figs with spiced balsamic
 syrup, 42

 strawberry tart with balsamic
 vinegar, 165

bananas: banana and passion fruit
 sorbet, 76

 banana ice cream, 63

 bananas in caramel rum syrup, 24

 caramelised banana bavarois, 97

 steamed toffee, banana and
 pecan pudding, 130

basil: basil syrup, 10

 tomato and basil sorbet, 77

basting, 216

batter: cherry and almond
 clafoutis, 115

 crêpes, 107

 fruit tempura, 116

bavarois, 92–7

 apricot and passion fruit
 bavarois, 93

 bavarois base, 92

 caramelised banana bavarois, 97

 espresso coffee and roasted
 almond bavarois, 97

 green apple and grapefruit
 bavarois, 94

 turning out, 93

binding, 216

biscuits: cumin shortbreads, 172

 hazelnut shortbreads, 172

 langues de chat, 173

 bitter chocolate truffles with wild
 honey, 185

blackberries: black and blue fruit
 sorbet, 78

 blueberry and thyme jelly, 31

blackcurrants: black and blue fruit
 sorbet, 78

 blackcurrant coulis, 12

blanching, 216

blenders, 215

blood orange jelly, 32

blueberries: black and blue fruit
 sorbet, 78

blueberry and thyme jelly, 31

bowls, 215

brandy: dark chocolate and brandy
 sorbet, 79

bread: baguette and butter
 pudding laced with Baileys, 126

 brioche loaf, 210

 summer pudding stacks, 163

brioche: brioche loaf, 210

 summer pudding stacks, 163

 tête à brioche, 41

brûlée, 216

brunoise, 216

brushes, pastry, 215

butter muslin, 215

buttermilk pancakes, 111

C

cake tins, 214

cakes: financiers, 173

 lemon and almond madeleines,
 178

candied fruits: nougat parfait, 67

caramel, 216

 bananas in caramel rum syrup, 24

 caramel sauce, 110

 caramelised banana bavarois, 97

 caramelised hazelnut chocolate
 clusters, 186

 caramelised mango slices, 42

 caramelised pear tatin, 142

 espresso coffee crème brûlée,
 141

 homemade honeycomb, 201

 slow roasted peaches with
 orange caramel sauce, 34

cardamom pods: cardamom ice
 cream, 58

 orange and cardamom cream,
 55

Champagne: strawberry and pink
 Champagne jelly, 28

cheesecake, pumpkin, 151

cherries: almond and cherry
 Pithiviers, 160

 cherry and almond clafoutis, 115

 cherry coulis, 11

 marinated cherries, 13

 peach and cherry trifles, 135

 tiramisu in two ways, 154

chestnut parfait, 68

chocolate, 182–9

 bitter chocolate truffles with wild
 honey, 185

 caramelised hazelnut chocolate
 clusters, 186

 chocolate and thyme ice cream,
 61

 chocolate chip ice cream, 58

 chocolate lady's fingers, 174

 chocolate macaroons, 176

 chocolate mocha tart, 148

 chocolate pastry, 203

 chocolate sauce, 131

 chocolate truffle croquant, 189

 chocolate truffle tartlets, 186

 coffee profiteroles topped with
 chocolate, 156

 dark and delicious chocolate
 torte, 164

 dark chocolate and brandy
 sorbet, 79

 little white chocolate and Kahlua
 soufflés, 103

 mango and dark chocolate
 mousse, 88

 melting, 183

 milk chocolate and nutmeg
 mousse, 91

 steamed chocolate pudding,
 131

 tiramisu in two ways, 154

 white chocolate and strawberry
 ice balls, 189

choux pastry, 205

 coffee profiteroles topped with
 chocolate, 156

cinnamon: apricot and cinnamon
 mousse, 91

citrus fruit: citrus fruit confit slices,
 47

 citrus fruit confit zest, 47

 citrus syrup, 10

 segmenting, 32

clafoutis, cherry and almond, 115

coconut: exotic fruit salad with
 fresh coconut, 23

coconut cream: Thai rice pudding
 with coconut and lemon
 grass, 132

My personal thanks must go to three very important chefs in my brigade: Mark Askew, the head chef at my Chelsea restaurant, who ensures the whole brigade marches to the same tune; Mark Sargeant for sacrificing his Saturdays off when he'd rather be biking on his super charged Yamaha; and Thierry Besselieure from Petrus in St. James', who helped me hone my pâtissière skills. To complete the team input, Ronan Sayburn, the sommelier at my Chelsea restaurant spent many hours perfecting words of wisdom on sweet wine suggestions.

Acknowledgements

I should like to extend my gratitude to everyone involved in the production of this book: to Georgia Glynn Smith for stunning shots, taken on precious Saturdays when she would rather have been with her newly wed husband – I'm flattered I mattered more on those occasions; to Helen Lewis for her chic artistic design that so complements my style; to Janet Illsley for gentle coaxing and professional editing; to Roz Denny, my co-ordinator in chief; and Anne Furniss, Quadrille's Publishing Director, for her continued faith in me. These may have been your roles, but it was service beyond the call of duty and you've all made it an exceptional book.

Roz Denny would also like to thank her many friends and relations who ate their way through the home-tested results. Their reward was the sheer pleasure in sampling each dessert. The team is also grateful to Magimix UK for providing the Gelato 2000 ice cream machine used in photography, and those suppliers who managed to obtain out-of-season fruits for photo shoots.